S/T

11-49

This book be
Claire Hamilt

THE
BOOK
FOR
NORMAL
NEU-
ROTICS

Books by Dr. Allan Fromme

Sex and Marriage

The ABC of Child Care

The Ability to Love

Understanding the Sexual Response in Humans

Our Troubled Selves

A Woman's Critical Years

THE BOOK FOR NORMAL NEU- ROTICS

Allan Fromme, Ph. D.

FARRAR • STRAUS • GIROUX
New York

Library of Congress Cataloging in Publication Data
Fromme, Allan
—The book for normal neurotics.
—1. Success. 2. Mental health. 3. Neuroses.
I. Title.
BF637.S8F68   1981   158'.1   80-25157

To
Some of my friends—my favorite normal neurotics

Betty & Nathan	Janet & Joe	Bert
Bobby & Bob	Joan & Fred	Frank
Cindy & Rick	Judy & Bob	Jaleh
Dorothy & Jess	Kristin & Joe	Neil
Elaine & Dick	Lynn & Steve	Richard
Elaine & Sidney	Margaret & Tom	Roz
Faith & Dariush	Nancy & David	Sally
Helen & Dick	Nancy & Jerry	
Jackie & Howie	Norma & Norman	
Jane & Jules	Pam & Lee	
Jane & Lee	Yvette & Tom	

Acknowledgments

The manuscript enjoyed the special advantage of Bob Markel's rare editorial skills. My own closeness to the material might have muddled it without the clarity of line he made possible.

As always, my wife makes any major undertaking a pleasure for me by the quality of her participation and her equally sensitive retreat, both of which have a nurturing effect on the work.

Contents

Introduction

What Is
a Normal Neurotic?

Probably most of the people we know—including ourselves
—are normal neurotics. What this means is that we're not
just one or the other, normal *or* neurotic, but both. Some of
us are more one than the other. Often we slip in and out of
these states as conditions around us vary. We have our bouts
with emotional problems and also enjoy periods of satisfaction and tranquility. We often have symptoms, but we're not
necessarily sick.

If we're not sick, what are we? What emotional symptoms
are we most apt to get? When are we really sick? When do we
need help? What can we do for ourselves if we're not sick
enough for help?

We ask these questions despite all we know today about
psychological illness. We still have difficulty helping ourselves. Grown children and parents scream at each other.
Husbands and wives tear at one another in fruitless confrontations. We wince at our shortcomings, real or imaginary. We
shudder at the advantage people take of us. We curse our
guilt but continue to feel its sting. We resent the rage of others but feel our own ripping our insides. Our sex lives remain
a fractional part of our sexual fantasies. Most painful of all,

we feel becalmed, unable to fulfill our potential and what we want for ourselves. Is it that we still don't know enough to help ourselves?

The fact is we know too much—*more* than we need but not *what* we need. It's the wrong kind of knowledge for us. We've learned what the psychologist has to know instead of what's good for the patient. Doctors have a great deal of medical information and make terrible patients. They're not even all that good at taking care of themselves.

What kind of knowledge should we have?

That's what I have tried to make this book about—remedies rather than explanations, solutions rather than descriptions. Most of us have been taught how we developed our emotional problems. And most of us still have them.

If we want to become *more* normal than neurotic, we must be shown how *to improve the quality of our experience*, not our thought. This is the way to counter the effects of our less than fortunate experiences of yesterday.

CHAPTER
1

How to Know Whether You're Sick or Healthy, Bored or Troubled

QUESTION: When does a person need help?

ANSWER: Generally, when he or she is unhappy and not functioning up to snuff. The trouble is that people aren't very clear about how unhappy they have to be or how poorly they're functioning before they really need help. Miss R., for example, admits she's sad a lot of the time, doesn't have nearly as many dates as she'd like to have; she's inhibited sexually so that at the age of twenty-four she still hasn't had sexual intercourse. In fact, she can't even bring herself to see a gynecologist. She gets along poorly with her mother. Still, she doesn't have any outstanding or well-defined symptoms. Does she need help? Or take the case of Mrs. N., age thirty-four, who's so terrified of getting into an airplane that all of the vacations with her husband have been no farther than a day or two away—by automobile. Despite the fact that she is a phobic personality, that is, fearful of many things, she seems reasonably happy. She has a good marriage, a fair number of friends, and few outstanding complaints about life. Does she need help anyway? Both these women can go on pretty much as they are—in fact, as most of us do—living

1

through the ups and downs of everyday life, winning a few, losing a few. Of course, many people improve their lives with outside help, short of being desperate. But it may be said that help is *needed* only when our own efforts fail to improve the quality of our experience. Generally this appears to us as being unhappy enough to *want* help.

QUESTION: How unhappy must a person be to want and seek help?

ANSWER: You know as well as I how that varies from one person to another. Getting help is ultimately determined not only by the amount of pain we feel but by our attitude toward help and the size of our pocketbook. It may sound crass but that's how it works. It's no different in medicine. Some people run to the doctor every time they have a cold, sore throat or upset stomach. Others, for one reason or another, go for years without seeing a doctor.

There are times when any of us need help and it would be a significant personal and social benefit for it to be available to us. There are times when life gangs up on us, when we wilt at the pressures we feel or become overly sad and unable to lift ourselves out of such states. There are countless ways our stability can be knocked into a cocked hat—a hasty decision, an unusually large risk, the sameness of each day or sometimes just ordinary fatigue. Any of these things can sadden us or make us wonder whether we're really capable of achieving what we want. In addition, there are predicaments in life that emerge out of nowhere, out of nothing we have done. There's no good reason not to get help at such times. Years ago doctors saw only sick people. The more important part of medicine today is preventive. One of the major reasons the beds in our mental hospitals go begging these days is that we recognize emotional difficulties so much earlier in life and treat them before they get so serious as to become almost untreatable. *Reaching for help doesn't necessarily weaken us and make us more prone to problems.* In today's enlightened times, a person needn't be seriously sick to get help. In fact, the willingness to seek help may itself be a sign of good health.

QUESTION: When is a person really sick, emotionally and mentally?

ANSWER: Okay. You're walking down the street and come upon someone standing on a street corner delivering a loud oration with many gestures but, as you get closer, you find not a single word of it is comprehensible. Of course, you know what everyone is thinking as they pass with a bemused or perhaps a saddened look. When a person's break with reality is that great and uncontrolled, it's clear that he's sick— seriously so. But then you get back to your office and find your boss raving and ranting, flushed, gesticulating just as wildly as the street orator, all about what you consider to be some relatively insignificant detail. Is he sick? You and I know that he isn't. *A person has not broken with reality if, when his emotions get out of hand, he is still comprehensible*, even if he exaggerates the importance of something.

In the course of our everyday behavior, many of us do stupid and crazy things. Needless to say, that doesn't mean that we are unintelligent or insane. In much the same way, we all behave neurotically from time to time. It might even be said that every individual has a neurosis. But when he's sick, the neurosis has the individual. This means that it has a more prevailing and general effect upon one's behavior. Mr. G., for example, believed deep down inside himself that his parents always preferred his elder brother. He felt they treated him like an "also-ran" and held him in little regard. He had lived with these feelings about himself for so long that even though he didn't like it, he was very good at this role. When he did something extremely well, he tended to regard it as an accident. If people praised him, he was genuinely uncomfortable with their praise. His shyness was an actual outgrowth of all of this and, as a result, he virtually invited people to treat him as though he were hardly there. It was as though he'd become so used to the shadows that, when the sun shone occasionally, he blinked rather than smiled.

Now, of course, this isn't nearly so dramatic or extreme as an uncontrolled break with reality. But it is a considerable misinterpretation of it. *All mental illness involves some misinterpretation. Therapy can most simply and easily be defined as a remodeling of attitudes, in which judgment becomes more realistic and feelings more appropriate to coping with what we judge.* This is more serious than it sounds. When you believe the wrong things about yourself or the people close to you or the world outside of you, all hell can break loose in your life. It can prompt you to violence and hostility when friendship would accomplish more. It can lead to discouragement when a little more effort would get you what you want. It can tax your relationships with people, blind you to opportunities all around you and be destructive in more ways than one can count. Misunderstanding breeds misunderstanding. As a result, a person's whole life can be so splintered and fractured by his unwholesome attitudes that his energies are drained by constant struggle instead of being freed so he can utilize his abilities in a way that would do him more good.

QUESTION: You mean to say a person is mentally ill, sick, neurotic, if he misunderstands certain things and feels disturbed by them?

ANSWER: The answer is absolutely yes. Of course, the attitudes and misunderstandings have to be significant. Many things don't matter. For example, a man who disparages professional football or boxing as subhuman, animal-like activities isn't neurotic if that's how he feels about it. Nor is a woman paranoid who is apprehensive about going out unescorted at night. One is a matter of taste, the other a not unreasonable assessment of the reality of the situation. If this man or woman reacted similarly, in this negative fashion, to *most* other things, then one might begin to suspect the possibility that something is wrong. You see, ordinarily we expect people to like some things and dislike others and be indifferent about still other things. We don't expect total negativism.

Some people may well have hostilities and fears built into them with which they approach *any* situation. They are not free to evaluate it as good, bad or indifferent. They are already bent in one direction. Changing their circumstances will not in any appreciable way alter their feelings about life. They go on a luxurious two-week vacation, find things wrong with the hotel, the food, the climate, the people, and so on and so on. They complain about the things around them, sometimes even with reasonable or just cause. But those aren't really the things that are making them unhappy. *When a person's reactions are predominately critical and hostile or apprehensive and withdrawn, then there is a reason to look further. In all probability, their attitudes have more obscure origins, relating to what happened to them earlier in life at home.*

QUESTION: Now you're saying that the things we complain about are not really the things that bother us, that our attitudes have deeper origins, that we don't really know ourselves. So, how can I tell if I'm neurotic and need treatment or not?

ANSWER: That's a fair question. It reminds me of the Quaker who said to his wife one day, "All the world's a little daft, save thee and me," but then under his breath added, "and sometimes I wonder about thee." Today, however, we've gotten to be so sophisticated psychologically that I think we worry not only about "thee" but about "me"—that is, ourselves too. We're beginning to recognize how some of the vague rumblings in our own discontent and poor performance may well be signs of chinks in the character of our overall adjustment. Again and again, we find ourselves returning to psychological articles, lectures, discussions, not merely because of our general interest in the field but because of what we suspect may be wrong with us which is correctable. So many of our friends are in therapy and talk about it that we no longer are terror-stricken by the idea that we too could use a little help. That's really the best answer to your question. It's not so much a matter of making a diagnosis—

"I am neurotic or I am not neurotic"—but, more prag-
matically, "Could I use some help?"

Here a brief inventory might help.

1. Are you still working on the same problems you were
   a year ago, two years ago, five years ago?
2. Are you still doing basically the same things about
   them?

If the answer is "yes" to both of these questions, then you
may need to be shaken up one way or the other. If you can
find a way to approach these problems differently so that
within a reasonable period of time you find yourself working
on other things, you don't need help. On the other hand if
you cannot do it, no matter how good your excuses are, you
need help.

Whether or not this proves beyond a shadow of a doubt
that you are neurotic is unclear, but that's not nearly so important as knowing whether or not you need help. *The point
is that we can need help whether or not we're neurotic and we
can be neurotic without desperately needing help.* For example,
a man can have arthritis—which is certainly an illness and, at
times, very painful—yet he can be happy. Additionally, the
fact is there may be no effective treatment whether he needs
it or not. On the other hand, another person can be physically
fit and yet need the services of an orthopedist because of the
extremes to which he presses his body in his athletic occupation. If all of this sounds confusing, it's because it is. The
important thing is not the label; it's the help we get to make
life better.

QUESTION: Very well, then, how can I know that I can be
helped?

ANSWER: Every age has its magic words. At one time it was
the Holy Grail, the New World, the West, gold, vitamins.
Today it's therapy! We're at a time in history when we place
great faith in therapy. The reputation of such a professional
effort is by no means unearned. Ever since the beginning of
this century, when Freud first made us aware of it, we've be-

come increasingly aware of previously unknown forces within us that tend to stymie and mislead us. Until the turn of the century, we hardly knew where to begin in the treatment of emotionally disturbed people. Now we know things about ourselves that people before Freud didn't even dream of. We know that a grown-up's perfectionism or how he spends his money can depend, to a significant degree, on how he was stool-trained as a child; that his feelings of optimism or pessimism depend on how he was fed as a child; that ultimately his love life may be largely a product of how his mother initially accepted him and then later weaned him away from her. True, these are things that are still challenged, but it is this kind of thinking which has alerted us to the continuity in our lives from the time we were infants on up to the present day. It has made it clear that we are a product of what we were. Our understanding is most enhanced by the realization that in each stage in our life we adjust to what is. Often we are not ready to give up what we have and, even more often, we are not ready to modify desires which we feel have not yet been adequately fulfilled. Many a child who feels insufficiently loved grows up to feel never loved enough so that there are women who have ruined perfectly good marriages because they feel their husband doesn't love them enough.

We know too that this is difficult for us to see in ourselves. This is why we have the faith in therapy that we now do. Somebody else, someone professionally trained, can see it more easily for us and not only help us develop these insights but, in some subtle way, steer us along lines that would be more rewarding.

QUESTION: I can understand that. But I know people who have been in therapy for years and who haven't gotten anything out of it. I don't want to become one of them. How can I know whether I can be helped?

ANSWER: Let me remind you of a couple of unhappy facts.
   1. The fact that the person is a therapist doesn't mean he's a good therapist. There are good and bad doctors

just as there are good and bad shoemakers or anything else.

2. The fact that a person goes for help doesn't necessarily mean he wants help, despite the hard-earned money he pays for it.

I mean "wants" it in the realistic sense. The person might
want something different from life when he applies for therapy, but he may be utterly resistant to *doing* anything differently for himself. He'd like to get along better with his wife and
spend more time with her, but can he help it if he doesn't like
art galleries, museums and the ballet? On a deeper level, he
feels neither responsible for nor able to change the fact that
his mother asphyxiated him with attention so that, without
even being sharply aware of it, he's more comfortable keeping his distance from any woman—even his own wife. He
genuinely wants things to go better at home, but remains
fixed in a mode of behavior designed to grasp and hold on to
freedom—not togetherness. He's going for therapy, but actually he's hoping for alchemy or magic.

So, first, in answering your question, it's important for you
to decide how realistic your desire is for help. Many people
go for the purpose of proving that nobody can help them.
Then they can retire into a life of self-pity justified by the fact
that they've gone to see several prestigious doctors, none of
whom could help. Needless to say, this is the way some neurotic people act. And you can't blame them! But what you
can do is to help them. This can be done by friend, doctor
and, most important of all, by oneself. A person has to work
his way back into good health—mental or physical. So go to
a doctor if you want to *work* at it, and get yourself a good
one.

QUESTION: How can I find a good doctor?

ANSWER: Unfortunately, there's a lot of circumstance and
luck involved in that. Most doctors tend to ply their trade
fairly narrowly. They do what they're trained to do. If a therapist is a psychoanalyst, he'll psychoanalyze you regardless of

your problem. If he's an advocate of drug therapy, the chances are he'll supply you with medication regardless of your problem. It's very difficult for you to know what kind of treatment you need. If you're lucky, you have a family physician who makes a good recommendation. If not, you've got to speak to your friends and have them speak to their friends. You can try to get information from the nearest university or hospital. When you finally see a doctor, the important thing is to go about it in exactly the same way that you would if it was some physical disturbance. You get a diagnosis and some indication of what kind of treatment is prescribed. If that sounds reasonable, you proceed with it. If not, just as you would do in the treatment of some medical problem, you go to another doctor to have it checked. It is extremely important to fight the passive tendency to put one's self totally in a therapist's hands without knowing what it's all about. It's easy for any of us, especially when we're troubled, to blur our judgment with the hope of stumbling on some superperson who's going to take care of everything. Commonly enough, the beginning of therapy often reveals such a "flight into health." We feel fantastic about the doctor of our choice and, after a mere two or three sessions, about life itself—only to discover, in a short while, it was the wish not the facts which generated our very temporary enthusiasm. A *realistic* approach will make you a better patient in addition to helping you make a better choice. You'll feel and act more like a participant in your own therapy and that is exactly how one should feel.

QUESTION: Perhaps, instead of looking for a therapist, making a change might do me some good. You know, get away from it all for a while. How do you feel about that?

ANSWER: I'm a great believer in change. Getting away from it all for a while is a good idea in general. We all need the occasional respite and refreshment of a new scene. The sameness of our everyday lives has a tendency to blunt our sharpness. There are few roles in life, regardless of whether you're a housewife, doctor, businessman, advertising executive, welder, stunt rider or judge, which fail to narrow down after a while to a point where you could almost write tomorrow's dialogue the night before. Even if we balance our daily lives with a variety of activities, we still more than occasionally yearn to spend a morning in bed or shoot a round of golf in the afternoon or just get away from what we've been doing day in and day out. But getting away is often disappointing because the change is diluted by the sameness we bring to it merely by being ourselves. The freer we are to adapt ourselves to a new situation and enjoy it, the more good it does us, but the less we need it. Generally, the more we need a change, the more that change has to be in *us* rather than in our immediate environment. If we could learn to do our work differently so as to avoid getting overtired or if we could learn to play differently, if our play has not been all that satisfying—these are the changes which would do us the most good. It would be therapeutic if we could do this. Maybe we can make some changes of this sort, or at least *try* to with somewhat greater effort.

QUESTION: Are you now saying that I don't need a doctor?

ANSWER: Exactly. Although I said earlier that everybody could benefit from help at times, I feel even more strongly that there's a great deal we can do for ourselves. Most of us are not so emotionally disturbed that we cannot help ourselves. It's difficult, but it's difficult with a doctor, too. Let's see what might happen with a doctor as compared with what you might do on your own. The doctor might advise against a vacation as a mere running away from your problem. I would most certainly not agree with that judgment unless you were discontinuing therapy, that is, not merely interrupting it but giving it up in the hope that a vacation would be more beneficial. Also there are times when you despair over not feeling any better despite all the time you've been spending with your doctor. She's helped you understand yourself better but you still feel locked in fear and indecision and life hasn't improved for you. Whatever the reasons for your behavior, there's still the sticky, hard-to-get-rid-of substance of habit. Now, instead, if at once—at this very moment—you do something different, however inconsequential it may be, you can start a process of loosening up, developing the flexibility that change demands. Read the last page of a book for no other reason than that you ordinarily don't do that when you begin a book, get up walk around the room and sit down in another chair. It need not be relevant behavior just so long as you start a process of doing things in a different way.

QUESTION: Certainly there must be more to it, isn't there?

ANSWER: Of course, this is the merest opening suggestion. The whole book is going to be about what you can do for yourself with or without a doctor. The whole thrust of this book is that if they're *your* problems we're dealing with, *you* must learn that it is *you* who is ultimately going to resolve them. Others may help, but only you can lick them. So you might as well start at once, even before you have a doctor. The emphasis is going to be put on what *you do* about your problems rather than how well you come *to understand* them. Once we learn to shift our emphasis from understanding to doing, the trick is to do those things which are good for us *habitually*. This is different from doing the things we like or think we like or think others think we ought to do. The idea is to let the end results speak for themselves. If, like the Lord, who looked at His work at the end of each day and saw that it was good, we're satisfied with what we did, we should do it again and again and again. We must learn to repeat what works for us. This emphasis on the end result of our behavior, on the bottom line, so to speak, exercises and strengthens our pragmatic ability to get results. We become less interested in our explanations and excuses and more focused on our rewards.

QUESTION: Are you saying just to let myself go and do whatever I feel?

ANSWER: Not at all. There are times when every single one of us is as wrong as can be about ourselves, about others, about life. I don't believe our feelings can be trusted all that implicitly. Just as there are times when every one of us feels the explosiveness of a four-letter expletive in us, so we feel like doing things which we know we'll regret later. I am not at all saying go out and do what you feel. I'm saying do the things that have worked for you and make every effort to stop doing the things that don't work, no matter how good your excuses may be. Let me illustrate what I mean. A woman I know works very hard. Gets a splendid job done at her office. She fairly frequently feels justified in leaving before five o'clock if she's finished her job, but always feels guilty when she sneaks out before the day is formally over. Just acting on her desire to leave early is not an unmixed joy for her because of the residual guilt. The trick is to find another way, to go about it differently. For example, she might actually tell her boss she is leaving early, that is, after she has already told him how much work she's put in on her own over the past weekend in order to get the job done so well in the office. It would be difficult for her boss to object under those circumstances and, after a while, unless her boss has some special hang-up on hours per se, he wouldn't at all mind that she comes and goes as she pleases because *she gets the job done*.

Now the unfortunate truth of the matter is that many of us *don't* get the job done as well as we might but still want to leave early. It's no wonder, then, that we are bugged about leaving early. Once we begin to emphasize what we do as opposed to what we know or think or feel, the quality of what we do becomes more important to us. As the saying goes "we cut the mustard." We know it and feel better. People around us recognize it too—which is a pleasant extra dividend.

QUESTION: Are you implying that life is one continuous struggle, denying ourselves the things we like and acting only on what is good for us?

ANSWER: It's a struggle only in those areas where we

haven't yet accomplished what I suggest. Once we learn how to do something in our best interest and repeat it, we turn it over to the "effortless custody of automatism"; and once it gets to be habitual, we no longer feel any effort. This boils down essentially to the difference between good and bad adjustment. The people who make things work just breeze along. Those who are not getting along constantly feel their wheels spinning, their gears clashing, their engine overheating —in short, great effort which is getting them nowhere. Don't you know people who, no matter how hard they work, are never finished? People who, no matter how much they earn, are always in debt? People who, no matter how well things are going for them, still complain and seem unhappy? Contrast these people with others you might know who, even in the midst of adversity, stay cool, confident and reasonably optimistic. Or people who do well with their earnings, stretching dollars even in inflationary times to yield real satisfaction for them. Or people who work hard, but not so hard as not to enjoy it. It's sort of like the good guys and the bad guys in the old grade B movies. There are those who seem in tune with the world as they work and rest and play: the good guys. Then there are the bad guys, for whom everything is a struggle—people, the world, themselves. Even when they get away with it and do well (for them), there's more pressure, effort, tension, in their lives.

No, I don't believe life has to be one continuous struggle, denying ourselves the things we like. Hard work is necessary, but not as an end in itself. It is ennobling, depending totally on what we work for.

It might be that what some people want in the first place is wrong for them or that the way they are going about it simply doesn't work. But if on the bottom line you're getting nowhere, repeating the same thing is deadly. Either new directions and/or new methods are imperative. It isn't that I want you to squelch your desires and feelings. I want you to satisfy them and then see what they do for you. This is what is meant by the phrase "live and learn." The trouble is we simply don't learn enough. Not totally because of deep, dark, inscrutable forces within us which tie us up into knots. The reason is much simpler. We tend to make the erroneous assumption that *wanting* something and *feeling a need* for it is motivation enough to get it. It may be motivation enough, but *achieving* anything is never the result of motivation alone. The whole point of childrearing is to teach the child the ways of the world. There are millions of causal sequences to be learned, so that we come to appreciate what begets what. The child is often helpless, merely putting its desires in evidence. The grown-up learns what you have to do effectively to fulfill these desires. You need to know the three Rs to live in an adult world; how to work, how to save, how to handle people; how to take denial, compromise and postponement; and, most of all unlike a child, that you cannot wish things into existence.

QUESTION: Okay, I buy that, but you made some reference to what I imagine are unconscious forces within us, inner conflict. Aren't those the neurotic elements within us you referred to earlier and wouldn't they make your program of action and change impossible?

ANSWER: Only in someone totally divorced from reality, namely a psychotic. Even neurotic people are capable of doing good things for themselves. And most of us are not even neurotic. Even if we are, we're essentially healthy neurotics. Sure, we all have our hang-ups, but there's still an enormous amount of control we have over ourselves. The question is, are we doing what we can? Are we utilizing our good health? If we don't do all *we* can for ourselves *without* help from others, there's a very good chance we won't do all we can for ourselves *with* the help of others. Helping ourselves, rather than feeling sorry for ourselves, has to become a way of life. It's a far more exciting way to live. The greatest danger is the passivity with which we give ourselves over to the uncongenial elements in our lives. The bona fide efforts we make to deal with them are fairly small and unimaginative and then we retire into the shadowy existence of rationalization and excuses for how unkind life can be.

QUESTION: Okay, I'm ready to look into ways of helping myself, but I'd still like to know whether I would be considered sick or healthy by a doctor; that is, whether I'm merely bored at times or really troubled. You've sort of answered it, but can you pinpoint it a little more for me?

ANSWER: Well, let me try. The problem is much the same as it is in physical medicine. The combination of hypertension and heart disease is our number-one killer and yet there are millions of people walking the streets who don't know whether or not they have either. There are even people under medical care who are known as ill, but yet how ill remains undetermined. No one's physical health is perfect. We all have an occasional stomach upset or cold, but we don't really regard ourselves as sick at those times, even though we might in fact take medicine. Yet if we took our temperature at any of these times and found it significantly above a normal reading, we'd probably get into bed. We do this not only because we feel weak, pained, uncomfortable, but because we're told that if we don't do this, we're going to get worse. So, are we sick when we catch cold or when we catch cold and run a fever or only with a full-fledged pneumonia? Strictly speaking, of course, we're sick with any one of these conditions, but it's only when we have to take it seriously that we call ourselves really sick. *We take it seriously when we lose the ability to function or are threatened by it if we remain untreated.*

The same is true for emotional illness. We all have our ups and downs. There are times we feel there isn't anything we can't do and times when we feel we are unable to get started at anything. We all have anger, hostility and hate, as well as love. At times we're courageous and at other times, fearful. But there is no simple procedure like taking one's temperature to determine if we're sick enough for treatment. The tests we have are very involved and complicated and require the efforts of a seasoned professional to make the determination. However, there are some general considerations which certainly help in our effort to assess the quality of our emotional adjustment.

We live our lives in five or six general areas and the thing to do is to determine how we function in each. The order in which we do this need not be important. Work occupies a good deal of any person's time. How well you perform there, what kind of promise for the future you enjoy in your work, how much you like it, are some of the basics. The same considerations should be made for the other areas in our life. In a society that stresses occupational achievement, we easily overlook the importance of play, another important segment of life. Many people simply don't know how to play. It's something perhaps they never learned or gave up and forgot once they reached their majority and felt the need to make a living. Sunday, for many people, is the most difficult day of the week. They look forward to it as the time they can do anything they want, only to find, when it comes, that they don't really know what they want. Unable to face this cruel truth, they justify wasting the day by claiming they're too tired to do anything. And this is only one of many pat rationalizations for failing to turn the day into a joyful one. Among other things, play ideally offers an opportunity to improve on reality by exercising one's imagination and fantasy. You don't have to be the best golf or tennis player in the world to feel that you just hit a couple of balls at least as well as they. Anyone who doesn't enjoy his play has to be unhappy and maybe is sick.

Family life is still another important area. After over thirty years of clinical work, I doubt I've seen a dozen people who have worked out their own emotional adjustment satisfactorily without having made some kind of peace with their own parents. This sounds incomprehensible to many. They point to the fact that there are people who simply are bad parents. True, they may be criminals or prostitutes but if they bring up their own children, emotional ties develop. I'll never forget a horrifying case of child abuse which demonstrated the strength of these ties. A ten-year-old boy, on returning from school one day, got into a fracas with his mother who, in a fit of temper, grabbed him and held his hands over the open range, virtually burning his fingers off. While he was being treated in the hospital, the psychological staff was asked to examine him and submit recommendations. The incident was so dramatic it had already come to occupy the front page of the tabloids. It was shortly before Thanksgiving and, after examining him, we hesitated to reveal the boy's urgent pleas to return to his mother. His request seemed bizarre, psychotic—but he checked out as normal. The court arranged to have his mother examined and subsequently kept under surveillance for a long time. Although the general reaction was one of dismay at the judge's leniency, I still remember the front-page pictures in several newspapers of the tearful, happy reunion of mother and child. Despite the fact that he had been treated that way by his mother, the child still wanted her. Needless to say, most of us as we grow older wean ourselves away from our parents and reduce their influence. But if we still get upset every time we speak to them, we haven't accomplished that to the degree we like to believe. We are not emotionally free. The weaning process has not yet been total and this, in turn, has an influence not only upon our own children and our marital partner, but even on our general social relationships.

Another important area is, of course, social life: having friends, many friends, and deriving satisfaction from their company, from the sharing of their lives and interests. All of this is an extremely important part of good adjustment.

Finally, we have a body which must not be overlooked. The old Romans used to talk about "a healthy mind in a healthy body." Today, of course, the influence of Oriental teaching has led some of us to believe that we can free our minds and emotions considerably, if not totally, from the body. Be that as it may, people frequently need activity and exercise just as they do rest. There are times I find myself too tired to keep my tennis appointment at the end of the day. But because I can't spoil the game for the three others, I go anyway and invariably find that after five or ten minutes on the court, I feel more refreshed than if I had taken a nap for an hour. Having literally sat still all day, my body needs movement. When we neglect the needs of the body, our mood is dragged down, our efficiency is impaired and before we know it, we're even snapping at people.

One of the most prominent of our bodily needs is sex. The quality of a person's sexual relationships cannot be over-estimated in any effort to determine whether a person is emo-tionally sick or healthy. We'll get into each and all of these things in the appropriate chapters which follow. Suffice it to say for the moment that a person is sick or healthy, depend-ing on how he performs and what rewards he enjoys in each of these areas.

QUESTION: I believe I can develop some rough estimate of my mental health. But I also mentioned that there are times when I don't know whether I'm just bored or afflicted with a more serious problem in not enjoying richer emotional ex-periences. What about that?

ANSWER: People in general don't regard boredom as an ill-ness. But, you know what? I do! Just as I regard laziness as an illness. If you literally don't use your legs, it's the same as being crippled, isn't it? If a man literally doesn't use his mon-ey, it's the same as being poor, isn't it? I regard boredom as a kind of illness because of what it does to a person. It deprives him of countless satisfactions, the fulfillment of which comes from the enjoyment of people and the active pursuit of rewarding interests. I always feel that a man is as rich as the number and vividness of his interests and friends. Addi-tionally, the person who is bored is virtually blind about him-self in at least one highly important regard. He says he is bored and calls things boring because, without seeing it, *he is boring*. He finds people dull because of the highly inadequate and bland stimulation he provides. He doesn't know how to elicit excitement from others. He doesn't know how, as a good teacher does—perhaps one you'll always remember—to invest even a dull subject with sparkle because of his own love and enthusiasm. Boredom, in short, is a state of emotional deprivation or lack of fulfillment which frequently borders on *dysfunction*, that is, the failure to utilize one's own resources and opportunities. But being troubled is another matter. There is a good deal of inner unrest and introspection that comes with being troubled. If the problems are external, one is supposed to be troubled and uneasy about these problems. If, on the other hand, most of the rumination is about oneself and one's inadequacies, the external problem becomes more personal and psychological.

QUESTION: Is that the time to get help, or only after reviewing the five or six categories of life you mention and finding my performance wanting?

ANSWER: The answer to both questions initially is *no*. You *need* help, but instead of rushing to get it, start by *giving* it— giving it to yourself. The chapters that follow will explain how you can do this. I am not averse to your getting help, but I emphasize the importance of starting by yourself. I repeat, a person who hasn't learned how to help himself *without* a doctor, all too often continues not to help himself even *with* a doctor.

CHAPTER
2

Useful Knowledge and Knowledge Not So Useful

QUESTION: I've got a friend who's really worked at helping himself. He happens to be smart, too. He reads every new book on the subject, he attends all sorts of lectures and courses in psychology. You should hear him talk on the subject. He's a real pro. Only he's still all fouled up. How do you explain that?

ANSWER: Today more people than ever know a lot about psychology and yet, despite that knowledge, they remain victimized by their emotional hang-ups. There are doctors who themselves have the very disease they are treating in others. People constantly make jokes about psychiatrists who, despite all their training and practice, are often "way out" themselves. The point is it's one thing to study psychiatry, it's quite another to study yourself. Your friend has unquestionably learned a lot about emotional problems, but he may not have learned much about *his* emotional problems.

QUESTION: But I also have a friend who's actually seen four different doctors in the last three years. You should hear *him* talk on the subject. He sounds even more like a pro than my other friend. Yet he too is pretty mixed up. If someone's learned that much about it all and still feels awful, what good is it?

ANSWER: Not much—until he gets to feel better. And he still might—sometimes therapy takes a good deal of time. You see, it's easy to learn things like the stuff you learn in school. That's almost purely intellectual, cerebral. It can even be done by rote memory. Therapy involves a minimum of that and, ideally, emphasizes what we *do* rather than what we think and feel. The fact is there are different kinds of knowledge and we have an unfortunate predisposition for the purely intellectual.

QUESTION: Different kinds of knowledge? What do you mean by that?

ANSWER: Your question reminds me of the little boy who one day was approached by his father, who had decided it was time for him to learn the facts of life. He went on for considerable time, waxing eloquent, talking at first about the birds and the bees and finally about human biology. The little boy sat patiently listening for some time and then finally looked up at his father and plaintively asked, "Dad, why are you telling me all of this? When I grow up, I want to be a businessman like you." The child's comments, of course, indicate his unreadiness for such information. But his father, whether he sees curiosity in the child or not, values information so highly that he dispenses it ready or not. This is what happens in school. All kinds of knowledge are dumped on us whether we see their relevance for our life or not.

Remember how you wondered why you had to learn physics, trigonometry, ancient history, and so forth when all along you knew you were going to go into your father's wholesale food business? But you couldn't fight it if you wanted to stay in school and so you learned and learned. At best, it was more decorative than helpful. Practical? No! In fact, as Thorstein Veblen pointed out, higher learning has been associated with the upper economic classes as part of their "unremitting demonstration of their ability" to be so free of the grubby business of making ends meet that they could spend their time totally on things that were of no practical value.

But when you stumble into a dark room, do you want a lecture on light-emitting particles or do you want to know where the switch is? When your car is stalled, do you want to know more about combustion engines or how to use a jumper cable and get it started? When you'd like a raise, do you want to know more about economic theory or how best to approach your boss? If you're a young woman planning a weekend at the beach, anxious to meet some men, would you attend a lecture on the reasons for alienation and estrangement in modern society or would you like somebody to tell you to get a very large book to carry around with you on the beach, bearing the title *Sex in America*?

This is what I mean by different kinds of knowledge. There's knowledge in general, and there's knowledge that works! Additional understanding of the reasons for a predicament just doesn't compare to some fact at hand, however superficial, which bears a more immediate relationship *to what you can do to be effective. When you need something, understanding isn't enough.* What we want, then, is what works! Many people enter therapy as though they were taking a course in psychology and, unfortunately, there are some who *give* therapy as though they were teaching a course in psychology. Helping yourself is one thing; educating yourself is another. I don't particularly recommend that my patients read books on the subject. I'm more interested in their reading good novels, journals of opinion, reviews of movies, plays, concerts—all for the purpose of getting them to enjoy themselves more and to make them more interesting people.

Worth emphasizing on the subject of different kinds of knowledge is how important it is to find answers that help. The father who teaches his child the facts of human reproduction rarely improves his sex life. Doctors, nurses, biologists, all know these facts, but they're not better lovers because of it. They have an intellectual, verbal grasp of the subject. This is one kind of knowledge. Another, more effective kind, minimizes the first kind while teaching the joys of sex under appropriate circumstances. That leaves us *feeling* better about sex rather than merely being more knowledgeable about it. Ideally, that is the goal of sexual instruction because, aside from procreation, sex is for love and for pleasure. Knowledge of the facts alone cannot help us handle our desires; appropriate attitudes toward sex will. Guilt and inhibition are greatly reduced not by collecting *biological* facts, but by learning *social* values that are more approving of relations between men and women.

QUESTION: I agree, but didn't you say that learning is worthwhile even if you don't use it?

ANSWER: Absolutely, I don't underestimate at all the fun of discovery and learning in itself. But here we are confronted with a very down-to-earth problem, namely, *what to do* about our emotional difficulties. In an equally down-to-earth fashion, I am saying that we have to learn what to do just as the problem reads. The psychological things we learn while studying the subject are immensely interesting, but unless they suggest clearly *what to do* about our emotional difficulties, they are essentially irrelevant. Let me illustrate what I mean. Ever since a freshman course I took at college, I have believed that the distance between the earth and the sun is approximately 93 million miles. Now, if in tomorrow's newspapers the headlines were to proclaim that astronomers have been wrong all these years and that actually it's 193 million miles, would I change my insurance policies, would I make a substantial withdrawal from the bank, would I stop having an English muffin for breakfast, would I do anything significantly different? Yes, if I were an astrophysicist I might have to go over certain other calculations and revise my opinions of related heavenly bodies. But as an ordinary citizen, it would have absolutely no effect upon me.

When we were children back in school and learned that Columbus discovered America in 1492, making the mistake of responding to a teacher's question on the subject by saying he did it in 1493 would make us look like second-class citizens. We would fail and be shamed. But I bet there isn't a teacher alive who can explain why it is historically significant that it be 1492 and not 1493. In short, we exaggerate the importance of much that we know and, in so doing, *begin to believe that knowing in itself is enough.* This is especially the case with psychological material. There isn't a straight man in the crowd anymore. Everyone today is so psychologically sophisticated that he is constantly judging and analyzing everybody else. And even if he were right, it would be unhelpful because modifying a person's behavior consists of enormously more than merely giving the person a diagnosis or explanation of it.

QUESTION: You mean that if you explain to someone that the reason he blinks is that when he was a child he used to get slapped often, that that wouldn't help him?

ANSWER: If you brought your overheated car to a mechanic and he told you, after examination, that your fan belt was shot, you would have, *at that point,* an accurate diagnosis, an understanding of the cause of trouble—but you would still have an overheated engine. Obviously, one has to act appropriately on the diagnosis, not merely state it, in order to get rid of the problem. Now in the case of your friend it's doubtful that the whole explanation or diagnosis has in fact been made. After all, there are many children who get slapped who don't blink. But even if it were true, it would still be unhelpful in itself. There would still be the years of habit to undo. Additionally, habits are rarely removed merely by knowing the reason for their origin. There is even the possibility that the person might blink more as a result of what you told him.

QUESTION: I would like to ask more about that but I also want to know more about the two kinds of knowledge. Can you tell us more about it?

ANSWER: Essentially, it's like the difference between a physicist and an engineer. The physicist explains the universe to us, but the engineer changes it, makes it more livable by putting the dams, the roads and bridges where they'll do us the most good. My reference to Columbus a moment ago reminds me that everybody knows his name for having discovered a whole new world. What we don't know are the names of the hundreds and thousands of settlers who made that New World the livable one that you and I enjoy today. Sigmund Freud, who was a giant in the history of this field, discovered a whole new world for us psychologically. But it is up to us now to use his material skillfully in improving our lives. A mere knowledge of the unconscious, of ambivalence, of Oedipal problems—none of that in itself helps us. Only as we adapt this information to our needs do we get to be like the settlers who made themselves comfortable in that new world.

We have a tendency to become fascinated with what we know and tend to use it literally. People believe they have to know everything about themselves in order to be emotionally healthy. To "know thyself" was a dictum of the ancient Greeks and more recently, when Freud pointed out how much we didn't know about ourselves, we got more interested than ever. I'm not here contesting the value of self-knowledge, but I do feel that we don't mean the same thing by the phrase "understand yourself." I don't believe self-knowledge requires the recapturing of infantile memories or the clarification of various unconscious forces within us. I like to think of myself as the ultimate pragmatist in suggesting that the best knowledge is the knowledge we can use.

QUESTION: I want to be specific on this point. What would be useful knowledge for our young friend who blinks?

ANSWER: Good question! It would be useful for him to know how to make himself more comfortable with others. Whether or not he remembers being slapped during his earlier years, certainly he knows—as does anyone today—

that we blink because we're apprehensive. What we're specifically scared of isn't nearly so important to know as the fact of our discomfort itself. Acting on this simple piece of information will help him more than digging for additional details of his early family relationships. Not that it's going to be easy in any case. Habits in general are hard to shake; involuntary movements are even more difficult because they employ muscles that are not under our direct control. Anything our blinking friend does to increase his pleasure with people and/or the quality of his skills will increase his poise and reduce his anxiety. Even if his blinking persists, he becomes less sensitive about it.

In short, we don't have to learn much. If we get heartburn from eating cucumbers and know it, we're not far from doing something about it. If we feel better after we lose five pounds and know it, we may not continue to act on it, but we're not far from doing more. We've got to learn what makes us feel good and what makes us feel bad. And the fact is most of us already know! The trouble is we underestimate its importance. After a man has had a heart attack and the doctor tells him to lose weight, he does. But he knew all along he was overweight and that it wasn't good for his health. It's just that he *knew* it in a general sense; but while he was symptom free, he never *felt* part of such a statistic.

One of the best doctors I ever knew, a great neurologist, used to say to his residents and interns on making rounds, "Don't talk so much, listen to the patient. Every one of them knows a great deal about himself. Unfortunately, he won't use what he knows. If you learn it, hopefully you will." Isn't it a pity that we need someone to help us use what we already know? It is true, isn't it, that the best advice we get is often what we've known all along? If there is anything we have left to learn, it's *how to do, how to act* on what we already know.

QUESTION: A little voice within me keeps whispering, "Haste makes waste." Isn't that a danger when you advise people to act this way? Mightn't we even make things worse?

ANSWER: Of course, there's always the danger of acting too hastily. But at such times we're acting impulsively and not at all on the basis of what we know. That's a bird of a different feather. There's a big difference between impulsiveness and being a doer.

The more important danger we face most of the time is that of doing nothing at all—thinking a great deal, turning the alternatives over in our mind, hesitating, being indecisive. These are the elements that make up the biography of most of us. We have an old saying in this business of clinical psychology, "I'd rather be wrong than doubtful." Doubt is not only painful but inhibits action. Nothing gets done and nothing changes. When we do something wrong, even though the situation is worsened, we feel more imperatively the need to change it and there is a good chance we learn from our mistakes. But if we learn from them at all, it is only *after* we've made them. We rarely learn from our *contemplated* but unperformed actions which might be in error.

If your question implies a request for a guarantee, it goes without saying that any promise of success is no better than any other promise. But just as they say one picture is worth a thousand words, it's equally safe to say that one act is well worth a thousand thoughts. Our good intentions may be initially pleasant to live with, but only our acts pay off. Those earnest thoughts that are not translated into action become the should'ves, would'ves, could'ves and might'ves that haunt us later on—the self-recriminatory ashes of earlier hopes. In the final analysis, *it's only what we do that gets up on the scoreboard.* This is the orientation toward life we must develop to improve it. To make case histories of ourselves may be a great intellectual exercise, but when you get right down to it, the only way we change our life is by doing something different about it.

QUESTION: Okay, but action isn't always that easy. Suppose you're inhibited; suppose your conscience keeps you from doing things you feel you ought to. Just as one person might act impulsively, another person might not be able to act at all because of having been brought up with certain moral prohibitions. Isn't that so?

ANSWER: True enough; as Hamlet put it, "Conscience doth make cowards of us all." Let's be specific. Take the case of the young woman who's been brought up to be "a good girl." She's very much in love, her sexual appetites are inflamed, she is aware of the fact that everybody else is doing it, she too wants to go to bed with her lover, but an echo in her past says "no."

It would be rash to tell her to forget it and to act as though these inhibitions weren't real. They *are* real. She isn't ready to make the jump from the ground to the tenth floor all in one giant leap. She needs a ladder.

She will have to do other things first. In order to develop the freedom of feeling and behavior she wants, she has to go through a number of preliminary steps. For example, she spends time with her lover wrestling with the problem, with her friends who are in various stages of solving the problem, with people who have a variety of views about it, even with movies and television shows that deal with similar situations.

Out of all of this, she begins to reshuffle her attitudes and feelings about it. In other words, we neither plunge into something precipitously before we are ready, nor do we dismiss it totally because we are not ready. We do little things like talk and think about it, while we sample the new activity to some degree. By taking it in bits and pieces this way, there's a good chance we may grow up to the reality of it all. The important thing is to become not one of those people who know, but one of those people who do. We talk and think about it for a while, but, to repeat, we keep sampling as well. We keep *doing*. And if we make a mistake in what we do, life is not so niggardly that we don't get second chances. But when we don't do, we don't even give ourselves a first chance.

QUESTION: But isn't it true that sometimes an experience we have can traumatize us? What I mean is that we do something that doesn't turn out right and then we remain afraid to do it again?

ANSWER: The people who are traumatized by an experience

that doesn't go right are almost always the nondoers who are quick to latch on to a reason not to act. My wife and I were in an air crash some years ago in which the whole crew was killed, many people were seriously injured, the whole plane went up in flames, but we were fortunate enough to survive without a scratch. The attitude we happily assumed immediately following it was that we must be indestructible. Of course, we knew that literally such a belief had no validity. We could slip on a banana peel and get killed the next day. But we haven't slipped on a banana peel, and believing that we are indestructible has helped us to fly hundreds of thousands of miles since, enjoying ourselves all the while. The point is that it's not merely the validity of any belief, but rather its function, its consequences for the individual who believes it, which is important.

If we were to accept literally the actuarial statistics on life and death, we would hardly dare venture to cross the street. Every four minutes somebody is hit by an automobile. Freedom comes from a happy combination of the facts and our imagination. Of course, it's a good idea to observe the traffic lights before crossing the street and it's an equally good idea to believe that you are observant and careful enough not to be an ordinary statistic. Part of good adjustment is an awareness and understanding of how the real world around you works. But that's only part of it. It's equally important to believe those things which have a freeing effect upon you so that you can move and act with both hope and conviction.

QUESTION: That puzzles me a little because many times I find the facts are disturbing or threatening. To develop beliefs that are freeing in the light of this may smack of wishful thinking. How do you reconcile the two?

ANSWER: Let's see if we can't evolve our answer out of some specific situation. Let's say you used to like to take a stroll after dinner on cold, clear winter nights. But now that you find the streets so emptied of people and you keep reading about muggings, you're frankly hesitant to venture forth. To develop the belief that you're different and won't be mugged would free you, but *would* be a case of wishful thinking. The fact is you're not different, that crime is on the rise and you are no longer safe in the streets at night. The statistics are against you—unlike my believing that I was indestructible following an air crash. At that time there was no increase occurring in the number of airplane accidents. My chances for a repetition of such an occurrence remained as low as ever, whereas your chances for being mugged remain as high as ever. Wishful thinking, in short, may be the kind of belief which frees you, but it does so *un*realistically.

I don't want to deny or abort the facts, but rather to use them in such a way as to support the conviction that you will be all right. I don't tell anybody not to cross streets. What I do tell them is how observant we have to be in the process. In that way, we can become confident as pedestrians or as drivers. Believing that we can do it—whatever it is—supplies some of the motive power for getting it done. But much of our belief has to be based on our awareness of the realities. It would be ridiculous for me to believe that I could make a go of my marriage just because I wanted to make a go of my marriage. It simply isn't enough. But if I combined that determination with an awareness of some of my shortcomings and an understanding of how best I could control them, then I would have reason for the development of some confidence about it.

QUESTION: I think I'm beginning to get the idea. I think what you're saying is that our feelings are important but so are the facts of life. I guess you're best off knowing a good deal about both. But isn't it true that we're often not sufficiently in touch with our feelings to know clearly what they are?

ANSWER: Absolutely. We'll see subsequently, in other chapters of the book as we get into the matter more fully, that we often fail to see how, for example, unloving we are. We see anger in other people but conveniently disguise it from ourselves so that, like the old joke, we angrily ask "Who's upset, who's upset?" referring to ourselves. But it's obvious to everyone but ourselves that *we* are. We're quick to place the blame for our distraught feelings on others. I've always felt *we either have scapegoats or symptoms*. Perhaps if we didn't blame others, we ourselves might suffer more acutely. But in shifting the blame, we might easily do the wrong things to correct our problems. Even more serious is the danger of not doing anything more than blaming others.

This points to the need for some self-understanding in order to work out our emotional difficulties. It helps to see things within us as they really are and call a spade a spade. Subsequent chapters will suggest how to get closer to our feelings. Suffice it to say for the moment, if we keep moving, we're going to be in better position to learn who and what we are than if we spend the time on the seat of our pants thinking about it.

QUESTION: There are many things about myself I know—but I still have a great deal of difficulty putting this information to good use, acting on it. Am I really going to learn how here?

ANSWER: I would certainly hope so. That's the whole purpose of this book. Believe me when I tell you I don't feel smarter than the next person on the matter of living life well. We all *know* a great deal about it already. It's not so much a question of adding to our knowledge as it is a matter of changing our emphasis. I hope to nag you, instruct you, cajole you, convince you, provoke you, beseech you *to act. Even doing the wrong thing is better than doing nothing*—within reasonable limits, of course. No one outside of a hospital or a jail is so blocked that he cannot do anything for himself. There are many things we can do.

Of course, there are psychological conditions that make it difficult. There is no doubt that inner conflict causes hesitation, delay, postponement. Fear often has an immobilizing effect upon us. Preferences and values inappropriate for our well-being can weigh heavily upon us and slow us down. Unfortunate experiences can thin out our motivation so that we easily lose speed and direction. But worst of all is habit. We are given to enormous repetition. *It is much easier to do the same thing again than something different, and this does us in more than we know.*

When we hear ourselves complain again and again, the time must come when we recognize that these complaints represent not merely our reaction to what is unreasonable or unfair in our lives, but that *they are our adjustment to it.* Justifiable complaints are complaints nonetheless, just as righteous wrath is wrath nonetheless. If we solved the problem, we wouldn't have it to complain about; nor would we continue to complain if we moved on more happily in utterly new directions. But no, we stay where we are, repeat what we do and complain about it. It is habit more than it is laziness and it is also habit more than it is inner conflict.

A woman may spend more than half her hour with me telling me how terrible her husband is. When I ask what she is doing for herself to make herself happy, she's stunned and resentful and invariably blurts out, "How can you expect me to make myself happy when my husband treats me so miserably?" My feeling is that if she literally cannot do anything to modify his behavior—though generally this is an avenue that she has not explored fully—she has all the more reason to try to do things with her own life.

No, we settle for things as they are more than we know. As a result, the difficulty we have in acting out a solution for any particular problem stems not so much from the problem as it does from our habitual tendency not to act. Of course, we don't like to see it this way, but it's only when we begin to believe this and make it an indigenous part of ourselves to take action on anything that doesn't please us that we begin to see results.

QUESTION: But aren't you saying, "Act on your problems even if you can't act on them"? Is that reasonable?

ANSWER: Yes indeed. If it's true that you cannot act on a problem that bothers you, then turn to other things and act on them. If the problem you turned away from is really important enough, it will reassert itself and force itself upon your attention. Only the same thing won't happen because if you have, in the meantime, turned to other things from which you derive satisfaction, you'll be in a far better frame of mind to work on the initial problem. Many times I feel that the best thing a person can do when confronted with some difficulty is not to rush out and try to solve it at once. The reason is that, in the throes of this newly emerged difficulty, he may be so emotionally upset that the action he takes is not in his best interests. It might be much better for him to regroup his forces, prepare himself by doing something that reminds him of his essential worth, his ability to win and to enjoy things. Then, when he turns to the problem, there's more he can call on in himself.

If I can recapitulate in part what I have been saying here, I've underscored the fact that, on the bottom line, only what you do counts. Your knowledge and intentions, however great, are reduced to sad decorative landmarks of what might have been if you fail to act on them—like empty excavations for buildings that never went up. The way we learn to act is by acting, by making it habitual. None of us solves all of our problems, but our percentage gets higher the more we do about them—the more we do in terms of acting on them, not complaining about them or studying them. We have exaggerated the importance of what we know, imputing to it almost the power of causal efficacy. But just as we all know more than we use about hitting a golf ball or a tennis ball, so today we all know a lot more about psychology than we use. The only way to change this situation is by practicing what we believe to be in our best interests. The practice itself has to become habitual. Like a concert pianist who spends hours at the keyboard even when he is not on tour, so we too have to keep moving in order not to lose our flexibility, our thrust, our habit of doing. Only this way can we translate what we know into our bodies and make it part of the language of our behavior. Only this way can we develop virtuoso status in the art of living.

QUESTION: But isn't it perfectly natural for people who are troubled to read about their problems? The media are full of psychological material. How can you expect us to pass it all by?

ANSWER: I like to think I'm realistic enough to know you won't. But what I'm presenting is not an either-or proposition. You can read all you like about the vagaries of human nature. No doubt it'll help you understand people and yourself better. That's certainly worthwhile and interesting. Only it won't free you of your difficulties. Understanding is for intellectual satisfaction, not therapy. In fact, it might even worsen the problem by misuse. For example, a man gives his wife a perfectly fine psychological explanation of why she overreacts to her teenage daughter's actions and she finds nothing but unmerited criticism in his "understanding" of her. There's an old saw in clinical psychology which suggests you find out what's in your patient's unconscious as quickly as possible, but don't tell him. He just develops stronger resistances. Even when we try to use our psychological insights on ourselves—assuming they're accurate—we generally wind up merely talking more impressively about ourselves or poignantly realizing that, for all we know, we still haven't altered our behavior or the emotional complexion of our life.

It's really not our fault. There's a good reason why it doesn't work; namely, *learning* about the psychological processes and experiences that shaped us one way or the other *is only an intellectual experience*. It's like reading about a riot, a hijacking, a mugging, which may, in fact, inform you more fully than if you were there. But it's not at all the same as having been there, victim of what took place. Even our own recollections of the experience, however full of feeling, remain mostly intellectual and fail to divest it of its effects.

QUESTION: Are you saying that even though our neuroses come out of the past, we don't have to go back and reexamine what happened?

ANSWER: The doctor does, but we don't. He needs a knowledge of our past to understand us well enough to direct us subtly into the kind of experience that can counter the effects of our earlier painful ones. Look at it this way: it's our *experiences in the past* that have made us what we are today—for better or worse—and it's only *our experiences today* that are going to make a difference. I repeat, *our experiences of today, not* our knowledge or recollection of our experiences of yesterday. The difference between the two is enormous and, like oil and water, they don't mix.

Most people, I daresay, believe contrary to this that if the neurotic elements in our feelings and conduct come out of our past, it behooves us then to resurrect that past. Don't we have to go back, think back to what happened? Why not? It seems reasonable. Even though the past is gone, it continues to affect us in a very lively way. But in another sense it's irretrievable. You simply cannot go back and get your mother (now dead) to pick you up at school to avoid the day she forgot; or your father (now also dead) to fulfill the strongly made promise of the bicycle you never got. You can recapture some of those feelings on the analytic couch, perhaps even help yourself to see something similar in your reaction to rejection today, but it doesn't change your reaction. Perhaps what you see is never more than only part of the story anyway. However tearful your recollection of initial causes may be, however classic your emotional catharsis and abreaction (reliving in memory), we cannot be sure that was really the cause or start of it all. After all, other kids had the same experience and shook it off. It might be that how someone began to be sensitive and easily hurt is not so important as what he himself subsequently did about it. Some people get tougher as a result, some get weaker; and in varying degrees we tend to lend ourselves, like the accident-prone person, to repeat performances of the major dramas in our life.

We cannot alter the past; we cannot have it to do over, but we can have an effect on our *tomorrows*. The way to come by this happy circumstance is through a shift in our emphasis. We have been emphasizing our yesterdays in order to understand. Starting with Charles Darwin who demonstrated in 1859 how well he could explain man by his origins, we have been explaining things by their origin ever since—all kinds of things. But just as every event has a cause (i.e., an origin) so it also has an effect (i.e., a consequence). Fortunately for us, *human behavior is just as affected by consequences as it is by origins*. This offers man his psychological salvation! Without it, he would be totally the result of everything that happened before he could help himself.

Let's see how such a principle can be used in our everyday life. A man may or may not know why he is so painfully sensitive to rejection, but he is relatively free to examine the effects or consequences of his own behavior on others. Certainly when he feels snubbed, the effect on him is to want to withdraw. He may simply not see the person who "rejected him" anymore. Or he may, but act so guardedly—expecting to be hurt again—that he appears untrusting. In either case, he could come to see—or be shown—how he himself is making a bad impression and, in so doing, is inviting more rejection. This is how we predispose ourselves and contribute to the "awful" things others do to us. Or we feel sorry for ourselves and say we can't help ourselves because of our crippling early experiences. But on the bottom line we're not getting what we want, which is to be accepted. The end result, the effect or the consequence is distasteful to us.

In order to change our feelings and behavior, let's first change our emphasis from origins to consequences, from beginnings to end results, from initial appearances to the bottom line and, most of all, from *why* to *how*. In short, we've got to learn to do something that no longer seems natural to us. But it's not natural to keep your eye on the ball either. It's natural to look where you want it to go. Habitually we have come to look for *explanations* of our behavior (in terms of origins) rather than *solutions* for the problems we develop in our behavior. This latter task requires constant awareness of the consequences of our behavior. Let the doctor look *back*; let us look *at*. And let us develop the habit of doing more and more things that provide us with the kind of *experience* we need to counter the effects of the unfortunate experiences of yesterday. Thought must finally yield to action. If we want to be more normal than neurotic, we must improve the quality of our *experience* much more than our thought. In the final analysis, the only thing that gets up on the scoreboard is what we do.

CHAPTER
3

What a Grown-up Is and How to Be One

QUESTION: By grown-up, in this context, you must mean someone who is *emotionally* mature. *Physical* maturity is easily enough recognized. Isn't that so?

ANSWER: Of course, you're right. As you say, we have little or no difficulty recognizing an adult in terms of age or physical stature. Whether or not that adult is grown-up emotionally is another matter. Often it's a very hard determination to make, and most difficult of all when it comes to ourselves.

QUESTION: I'm sure you are going to tell us why it's important to achieve this state and to recognize it. Yet I must confess there are times I wish I were a kid again, free of responsibility, living a nice, easy life.

ANSWER: We tend to romanticize childhood and forget the grief we suffered growing up. It's not at all as good as we like to remember it. Even then, we weren't entirely free of responsibility and we weren't very old before we began to feel the yoke of restriction and the consequences of our own ineptitude. Our lives were anything but free because our choices

by and large were made for us. But good or bad, different things are expected of us as we get bigger. We couldn't continue to live as children even if we wanted to. The trouble is we cling to what we *were* more than we know and this makes it more difficult than it need be to live in a world of adult expectations.

QUESTION: There you go again saying that even though we know better, we hang on to something that doesn't work for us. Do you really believe we remain children in many ways?

ANSWER: Nobody grows up without getting rid of the child within him. Only we don't do it totally. In the same way, nobody has perfect health or perfect anything else. The more mature we are, the less childlike we are. That's obvious, even by definition. But not all of us are equally mature. Additionally, being mature doesn't guarantee that we will act on the same level of maturity all the time.

QUESTION: I know you're right, but I want to be thoroughly convinced that what children are like won't work in an adult world. Can you spell that out?

ANSWER: Sure. Let's begin by reminding ourselves what the outstanding characteristics of children are. This will help us see:
1. How inappropriate their feelings, thoughts and behavior are for the demands of adult living, and
2. The residual elements of childishness that remain in our own behavior.

First, though not necessarily in order of importance, I think you'll all agree that children are naive and inexperienced. Grown-ups are knowledgeable; they know the ways of the world and they have a sense of causation; that is, they know what causes what in life. Thus a child, strongly tempted to reach into the cookie jar, doesn't pay enough attention to getting caught, and it takes him even longer to believe that he isn't going to be forgiven. A grown-up generally

is not so naive as to believe that if he puts his hand in the government till by underreporting his earnings, he's going to get away with it as easily and will be forgiven. Instead, he uses a more knowledgeable or sophisticated approach to the same thing by consulting with a tax lawyer or an accountant to find what legitimate loopholes in the law exist of which he can take advantage. The simple and wishful thinking of the child won't work in the adult world.

Secondly, children are for the most part dependent. For many, many years there is very little they can do for themselves. Now although nobody is so totally independent as not to require specialized help, grown-ups essentially look after themselves and, as a result, are free to make their own choices. Third, children have a very short attention span. They really can't stay with anything long enough to achieve very much. The need for some kind of significant achievement is overwhelming in adult life and without perseverance one couldn't expect it.

QUESTION: I realize that a child, no matter how brilliant, couldn't make it in our adult world. It's too complex. I was going to ask something else, but are there still other characteristics that you were going to mention?

ANSWER: Yes, just several more. Children commonly lack control over their own desires so that they are often trapped by them. Little Mary, for example, cannot understand why the ice-cream cone she wants has to be put off until after dinner. She fails to see postponement, only denial and rejection. Since she is unable to enjoy the partial satisfaction of promise, her desires often swell out of control because of their imperative, now-or-never quality. A grown-up understands that need for postponement, compromise, even denial. That's one of the biggest differences between a child and an adult. A child cannot take "no" for an answer without smarting. As a result, there's still another major difference between children and grown-ups. Whereas grown-ups enjoy relative stability, children have emotional ups and downs all of the

time. For most kids it takes six years before they spend their first cryless day.

On another level, a major difference between children and grown-ups is a matter of values. An adult is expected to have developed an *appropriate* sense of values; children, without the keen sense of time their elders enjoy, tend to see things only in their immediacy. Only that which is tangible and exists before their very eyes has value. Their perception is dominated by the moment, and as a result they cannot, in fact, provide for anything beyond today's satisfactions. Tomorrow —the future—doesn't exist for them so that they have to solve the same problems again and again. The child is like primitive man who, before he figured it out and domesticated cattle so that he had a constant supply of meat, had to go hunting almost all the time—and frequently went hungry.

QUESTION: What I was about to ask a moment ago was: you don't literally mean that all adults have these characteristics that you mention as different from those of children, do you?

ANSWER: Oh no, of course not. These are characteristics of adulthood or grown-upness. On the average, you'll find them in greater abundance among grown-ups than among children. As I said earlier, the *more* grown-up we are, the *more* do we act this way. But it goes without saying that we all have chinks in our armor and behave like children at times.

QUESTION: That's what I want to get to. Why?

ANSWER: Essentially you're asking why we don't grow up perfectly adjusted or perfectly mature. It's common knowledge we're not all treated the same way as we grow up. We are not all equally lucky (or unlucky) in the kinds of parents, homes and experiences we have. Children, for example, who are brought up in homes where the parents are themselves fairly naive and inexperienced, or have large elements of dependency in their makeup, who have little control over their own desires, who have huge emotional ups and downs, are willy-nilly taught by these parents to be immature. Most people, of course, are brought up by parents who try to help but cannot beyond the boundaries of their own limitations. As a result, these shortcomings get passed on from parent to child. But it's not an all-or-none matter. It's not merely black or white. There are many shades of grey in between. People are immature about some things and fairly grown-up about others. Because of this, we turn out differently from each other in the way we behave.

QUESTION: I guess you're saying the apple doesn't fall far from the tree. Is that right?

ANSWER: I'm saying that, but not in the sense in which that phrase has generally been used. People used to say that when they spoke of hereditary influences. I don't mean that the degree of maturity that we achieve is an innate characteristic.

QUESTION: But wouldn't you say that a more intelligent person has a better chance to achieve maturity?

ANSWER: Not really. Granted a person of subnormal intelligence would remain dependent throughout his life, yet a person of hugely superior intelligence might spend so much of his life involved in his work that some of the ordinary demands of adult life might escape him. By and large, emotional maturity is not a product of intelligence. The more intelligent we are, the more skillfully we may be able to *conceal* our emotional immaturity. When a child uses big words, people say he's precocious. He may actually be emotionally immature for his age but verbally or intellectually precocious. In the same way, there are many adults who sound very grown-up because they talk a good line. But their emotional life may be a shambles, and may always have been. No matter how intelligent they sound, their decisions are naive and they may need other people more desperately than they dare put in evidence.

QUESTION: I want to get the clearest possible picture of childishness or emotional immaturity in adults whom we generally recognize as pretty grown-up. Can you give me some examples of that?

ANSWER: Yes indeed. I think it might be instructive. Let's start with the case of the young woman who has been hotly pursued by several suitors, among whom she finally makes a choice. Amid great fanfare, they marry and soon settle down to a life together. Much to her dismay, she soon finds that the man she chose, who was the most attentive, demonstrative suitor of the lot, spends Sunday afternoons watching professional football games, half of Saturday playing tennis, stays late at the office, is often tired and grumpy when he does get home, hates going to galleries and art museums, and that even their sex life lacks the passion that it had at first. Unhappy, she complains constantly to him and has seriously begun to doubt the wisdom of her choice.

QUESTION: You mean she's immature for being upset under such circumstances?

ANSWER: No, I don't fault her for feeling bad. Her immaturity shows more clearly in what she's *not* feeling and doing about her problem. Remember, I said children are naive and inexperienced. They don't know the ways of the world, they don't have an adult sense of causation, they're not knowledgeable. This describes our young woman's reaction. If she were emotionally grown-up, she would know that you don't simply make a choice in life and then sit back and reap the benefits. A good choice, as compared to a bad one, essentially gives a person the opportunity to work at what she wants. In a bad choice, no matter what you do, it doesn't help. But all she is doing is complaining. She is dismayed, instead of knowing that millions of men stay late at the office, spend Sunday afternoon playing tennis, don't like art museums, and the rest. Because he loves her, she has a great opportunity to make inroads into his life and alter it so as to get more of what she wants. You never just *find* that. You have to *create* it. But she has little or no motivation to do so because of her overevaluation of the importance merely of the choice. Children cry if they don't get everything they believe they were promised. Grown-ups may feel some disappointment too under such circumstances, but more realistically they focus on what they can do to change things for the better.

QUESTION: Wow! I begin to see how many grown-ups I know who maybe aren't so grown-up all the time. Tell me more?

ANSWER: All right, let's take the case of a high-energy, fast-talking businessman driven to make a fortune. You regard him as extremely knowledgeable. He's always into something big. But his fortunes and his emotional life seem to be on a constant roller coaster. There is always some huge deal that falls through at the last moment, or a killing in the market, or a lawsuit that ties him up for some time, or an investment of great promise. But on net balance, he is more often than not cash hungry, servicing huge debts, living beyond his means, constantly placing his equity in jeopardy, leading a frenetic life involving excesses in both drinking and eating, so that he is overweight, hypertensive and, although he might have flair, friends and drama in his life, he has little peace, security and stability.

QUESTION: I know exactly the type you're talking about. You regard such people as immature, I gather?

ANSWER: Yes, I do. Although such a man claims it's in the nature of his business to be so pressured, it is actually he who is introducing the emotional ups and downs and pressures because as soon as he has some security and can enjoy some stability and peace, he feels like a child cooped up in an apartment on a rainy day. He has activity needs, in short, more like those of a child than of a grown-up. He can't sit still. Additionally, despite all his experience, he keeps making the same mistakes again and again. Surely he knows a great deal about business and yet he allows himself to get overly excited and involved in deals which any experienced person must know are basically long shots. On top of that, he has about as much regard for his money as a child does for its toys. Instead of caring for his capital, he exposes it repeatedly to jeopardy and then winds up in debt, once again dependent. All of this leads him to excess, to the point that endangers even his physical health. It is as though he needed somebody to take care of him.

QUESTION: I see what you mean. It's very easy not to recognize immaturity, even though it's there, isn't it?

ANSWER: I'm glad you put the question as you did. The game or life-style this man is involved in is available only to grown-ups. The amounts of money involved are not available to children and so we're easily deceived. But grown-up games can be played in a childish manner, just as a person can express very immature feelings with a highly grown-up vocabulary. I should add that I don't mean to give the impression that a man with an "iffy" financial career is necessarily immature. And conversely, huge financial success in no way guarantees the emotional grown-upness of anyone. When we read about these people, we tend to impute it to them just as we do to socially prominent people, politically prominent people, in short, people who are outstanding in any area. We do this because achievement is highly valued in our culture. We are driven by the Nietzschean principle that "I am that which must ever surpass itself." The point is that success and prominence are the complex results of many things ranging from luck to ability, and very often reflect a person's emotional strengths or weaknesses only to a minor degree.

QUESTION: Well, if that's so, why make such a fuss about the importance of emotional grown-upness? If we can be successful without it, why pay much attention to it?

ANSWER: Your question might be hard to answer because of the extent to which most of us hunger for success and prominence. But we must be reminded that "the boast of heraldry and the pomp of power," no matter how appealing, don't guarantee our satisfaction with life. Although it may be hard to believe, a man can be satisfied with his success and yet dissatisfied with his life. Many socially prominent people are worn out by their prominence. And there are many successful people who feel driven and almost enslaved by their success. They often feel that they have sacrificed their family and home life for it.

QUESTION: I see what you mean. But could you give us some simpler examples of immaturity in our everyday behavior?

ANSWER: Yes, I think I should. Perhaps you remember that I mentioned a while ago that one of the major differences between a child and a grown-up is the ability to take "no" for an answer, that is, with emotional equilibrium. Okay, you phone some young woman you know for a date, she says "no" and you go to pieces. You decide she doesn't at all like you, she'll never say "yes," you'll never call again and you feel pretty glum about it. You may be very grown-up about other things, but this is the way a child reacts when refused something. The only difference is that the child expresses his feelings, the same feelings, overtly—by crying. How would a more mature young man react to being turned down? By deciding that the next time he asked for a date, he would offer something that couldn't as easily be refused: theater or ballet or dinner or even just a more interesting line of chatter before suggesting the date. He does this precisely because he doesn't want to be rejected and feel bad a second time. A child doesn't work for what he wants. He merely asks for it. Grown-ups make it habitual to work for what they want and that's how they get it. I think it's safe to generalize that almost any overreaction to disappointment is fairly immature. It's not that we don't feel the chagrin of disappointment as grown-ups. We feel it all right, but we get cracking on another tack that promises greater success. In short, we don't merely sit and stew and feel sorry for ourselves. Children do this because when someone says "no" to them, they have little recourse. But as grown-ups, we have resources, experience, ingenuity, know-how, perseverance and so we put it all together to achieve our ends in some other way.

QUESTION: Okay, I'm beginning to see more clearly the value of being grown-up and mature. It's kind of like being in better control, wouldn't you say?

ANSWER: Exactly. Grown-upness does offer better control —but not total control. Nobody has that. There are forces bigger than us and we can't win 'em all. So part of grown-upness is to learn how to lick one's wounds and move on to other goals. It's like the song that goes, "If you can't be near the girl you love, then love the girl you're near." Of course all that's easier said than done. But the point is that the mature person keeps his eye on target—that being what's in his best interests. We can't always have what we want, no matter how ingenious or energetic we may be. And it's important to know that there are always other things we want that we simply haven't yet considered.

QUESTION: You're sure that's not a put-off or rationalization?

ANSWER: It can be very easily, but it doesn't have to be. If there has been no additional effort and inventiveness, then it may be as invalid as any sour grapes story. But if you've really worked at it and your efforts don't pay off, at some point it's the better part of wisdom to modify one's goals.

QUESTION: Your use of the term *wisdom* suggests that maybe that's what emotional grown-upness is essentially. What do you think?

ANSWER: I suppose so, except that I don't care for the intellectual emphasis in putting it that way. I feel that grown-

upness or maturity involves much more than specific understanding of situations. It's more a matter of what we do about
them—more a matter of what we do about our feelings as
well. This, of course, brings us to the question I was sure you
were going to ask, namely. . .

QUESTION: I know: how do we go about improving our
own emotional grown-upness?

ANSWER: That's exactly what I want to talk about. I've said
repeatedly in this book—and I will continue to say it—that
the only way we make a difference in our whole psychology
is by what we do differently. Getting answers, however
learned, getting insights, however revealing, setting new
goals, however worthy, or making resolutions about one's
feelings, however well-intentioned—all this by itself is
doomed to fail. We don't reliably learn to act differently as a
result of any of these things. I know this is a strong statement,
but I yield only enough to admit that very little thought and
feeling influence what we do. For the most part, it's the other
way around. The way we feel and the way we think are much
more often the result of how we act—or how we haven't
acted. Additionally, it's much easier to alter our behavior
than it is our complex, devious and labyrinthine thoughts and
feelings. You can tell a person simply, "Walk into that room
and smile even though you're scared and unhappy," and he
can do it whether he wants to or not. He might feel better for
it and even come to think differently as well. Or you can tell
someone you don't blame her for being both angry and depressed as a consequence of her boyfriend's failing to show
up. But to sit and talk about it all night doesn't compare in
therapeutic value to dragging her out for a brisk walk, a
snack and maybe even a movie. The activity will improve this
young woman's mood, and once improved, she'll more easily
see what's been amiss in her behavior with men and her
choice of them. Telling a person not to worry or feel bad or
that his pain isn't serious or that he must dredge up things
that happened when he was a child in order to see them dif-

ferently—all that can take forever. At the same time there is little guarantee that once he does, he'll feel better and act differently.

QUESTION: I know you're about to tell me to act differently with members of the opposite sex or my parents or some of my co-workers. I know that would be valuable for me but I can't do it. And I'm aware I can't because of attitudes and feelings I have about them. Aren't you expecting too much of me?

ANSWER: No. You're not expecting enough of yourself. It's simply untrue that you *cannot* act differently with any of these people. The truth is, you *haven't* acted differently—but you can. Of course, there are things that stand in your way, such as your pride, your affections and disaffections and, most of all, your habits of behavior. But none of this is insurmountable. When you claim that it is, you're implying that changes in your behavior can only come as a result of the changes in the behavior of the people in the world around you. That's flatly unreasonable. Short of this, the only other way you can possibly come to think and feel differently about them would take years of therapy. I believe you can do it in much less time yourself. Granted there is an element of knowledge involved—and not much more—and I can give you that in a nutshell.

1. Keep your eye on target—target being that which is within your best interests.
2. The only thing that gets up on the scoreboard is what you do.

Let me illustrate what I mean. Joan and a girlfriend decide to go to a concert two weeks off and Joan buys the tickets. They weren't especially costly, the seats being nearer the ceiling than the floor of the hall, and her friend was to buy dinner. At two o'clock, the day of the concert, her friend calls with some lame excuse and backs out. What would you do? You're stuck with the tickets, you're disappointed, you had turned down other arrangements for the same night, you're

geared up and ready to go and you would be perfectly justified if you blew your cool. But justification doesn't get up on
the scoreboard. It's only what you do about your dilemma
that counts and it's only what you do in your best interests.
That would be to make a date with her then and there for
another night! Then, on getting off the phone with her, immediately call all the other people you know. In fact, you
could speak to some people in the office you don't know so
well whom you might like to know better. You could be a
sport and invite that attractive young man down the hall.
He's the one you heard whistling something from Bach. Such
behavior is directed toward the simple goal of getting to the
concert, which is what you want to do. You might not only
come up with a better evening, you might even make a new
friend. Granted you might not. You might lose and find no
one. But I can guarantee you that making that kind of an
approach habitual will bring you many rewards in the end.

QUESTION: But if your friend's excuse was a lame one,
doesn't she deserve to be bawled out?

ANSWER: Sure, but why should you do it? It's not in your
best interests. All you could get out of that is the small
amount of vindictive satisfaction that comes from blowing
off steam. She's not going to thank you for being bawled out.
She will thank you for giving her, right then and there, a
chance to make another date, which is tantamount to for-
giving her. We don't benefit by rubbing people's noses in
their own shortcomings. They already suffer from them by
themselves. Your best interests are served by making other
arrangements and spreading goodwill. That leaves *you* with
the option of continuing your friendship with her or not.
Bawling her out may encourage her to drop you. The fact
that you like going to a concert with someone doesn't mean
that you like everything else about her. And it's much easier
to go through life letting people be what they are than to go
about trying to change them.

QUESTION: Once again I feel that you might be expecting too much of us. Don't you think so?

ANSWER: Not really. I didn't say you shouldn't *feel* disappointed. The word *should*, incidentally, is the biggest weasel word in the English language. We can't always arrange what should happen; we are bound to get disappointed sometimes. The important thing is to take action at once—to do something about it—so that instead of sulking and brooding, we can once again give ourselves the satisfaction we were promised. Needless to say, things of this character will keep happening to us countless times. But the more we practice this, the better we get at it. I know how hard it is, but it's hard to develop any new skill or improve a skill you already have. It takes enormous concentration and repetition. We all have bad feelings that are easily ignited. Why drop everything else and concentrate on the bad feelings? Why allow them to envelop us, to possess us? It doesn't have to be that way. There are loads of important things we do every single day in the week that we don't want to do—brush our teeth, comb our hair, put on a necktie, get to work on time (or almost), be pleasant to the boss, deny ourselves things we can't afford, and so on. We do them because basically we know they're in our best interests and a necessary part of adult life.

QUESTION: It's a big order but I must admit it makes sense. I never realized how much we live with our thoughts and feelings and how little we focus on our behavior. Now, are you saying if I work on this habit, I'll get to be more grown-up emotionally?

ANSWER: Absolutely. Just think—unlike a child, you'll learn how to take "no" for an answer more easily because you'll become more adept in working things out with people instead of sulking like a child and feeling sorry for yourself and being utterly dependent upon the reliability of people's interest in you. You'll *create* the circumstances that make their interests coincide with yours. All of this contributes to far greater emotional stability because you won't be buffeted about by mood swings touched off by the tiniest untoward response from others. You'll feel better more of the time as a result of all of this so that you can think more clearly and enjoy greater confidence in the solutions you develop for the daily problems of living. That is what we mean by being grown-up. But I warn you, it takes lots of practice. Don't be discouraged by early failure. It's an enormous transition from wallowing in our feelings to *acting* habitually. This is not an argument against the value of thought. As a matter of fact, you can't argue thought out of existence. But we all think better on our feet. Thought is best when it's reflective. The more behavior we have to reflect on, the sharper the comparisons we can make. It's when we sit alone in the corner and try to solve the problems of our life that we get into trouble. That easily gets to be an unending morass of bias, contradiction, blindness and emotional upset. When the things we do work, we'll see it. It's an easy perception and the thought that follows does not take great genius: namely, do it again. Like a good athlete, we develop elements of grace and timing in our behavior so that even while we are accomplishing more, it seems to get easier all the time.

CHAPTER
4

Psychological Necessities
We Tend to Forget

QUESTION: Do you mean by a psychological necessity our need for love?

ANSWER: Not quite. We're generally aware of our need for love and talk about it almost as often as we do about money and opportunity. We have other psychological needs important to our well-being which are *not* nearly so obvious and, as a result, we don't really work deliberately enough on them.

QUESTION: Offhand I cannot imagine what they are and, at once, I wonder if I'm neurotic not to know them.

ANSWER: Not at all. Well-adjusted people also overlook them. The result is that we tend not to do enough about them. After all, nobody's perfect.

Take our need for change—a break in our routine—as a case in point. Even though it's imperative, I feel, we only sporadically recognize or talk about it—and do something about it even less often. One of the simplest things that dulls the sparkle of life is the *sameness* of so much of it. Allow me to propose a small task: that we sit down tonight and see if we can write tomorrow's dialogue. Try it—really. You'll agree we know whom we are going to see, what we're going to say, what they're going to say, what we're going to do next, what they're going to do, and on and on. The task was not very hard. Reason: we spend countless days and nights monotonously repeating the pattern of each yesterday. To a large degree, this is expected of us. Our jobs demand it. It's what we get paid for. The idea of doing anything else becomes so far removed that it seems to take only the wildest stretches of our imagination to break the pattern. Just think, what have you done for the last six Saturdays or Sundays in a row? How are the days of the week different from each other for you?

More than we know, this sameness dulls our perception and the emotional tone of our life. As we repeat ourselves, we become so much more efficient at whatever we are doing that less of our attention is demanded. When you first get a new car or television set, you fiddle with the controls, admire the details of its construction and enjoy a certain sense of aliveness in the keener attention you give the new instrument. As you get used to it, you hardly notice it and everything you do with it is turned over to the effortless and automatic mechanism of habit. The more things in life we do this way, the less sensibly alive we are. Days go by with little or no elevation in feeling. After a while, we even become somewhat detached from ourselves. Our language, mirroring our lives, lacks the zest of superlatives, sensitivity and excitement. Who knows— even an occasional outburst of hostility may be good for us!

This is all more serious than it sounds at first. As we suffer this creeping anemia of the emotions, we begin to feel more habitually bored, tired and depressed. Now comes the most serious part. The zest and excitement in our lives at best becomes more and more vicarious. Science fiction, horror films, violent sports, TV cops and robbers, become our daily fare. The fact that such entertainment is so popular testifies to the enormity of our need for excitement and, simultaneously, to our failure to manufacture it in our own lives. Not that we fail totally. We do things directly with ourselves also but, unfortunately, fairly harmful ones. We drink too much, drive our cars too fast and, all too often, abuse ourselves with drugs.

Still another harmful consequence of the detachment from our own feelings that sameness in life produces is the overall weakening of our ability to cope. Human relationships in general and marriage in particular are areas where this fact is most prominently put into evidence. The person who is bored, tired, mildly depressed, unfulfilled, lacking excitement in his life, is the same person whose motivation for anything gets so thin, he comes to expect less. His hopes, even his dreams, eventually fade. He seems to lose the energy to work on changing things he doesn't like about his life and, in failing to make the necessary changes, he leaves himself only with the extremes of alternatives, either dully to accept *what is* or merely to walk away from it. We tend to walk away from our relationships, not just marriage, more easily today. It's not the shortcomings per se in friendship or marriage which make them short-lived, but our failure to work on them in order to iron out some of the inevitable shortcomings people bring to these relationships.

QUESTION: I can see how we allow the sameness of our lives to dull us, even making us depressed and sad. What can we do about it?

ANSWER: Once again, the magic word in your question is the word *do*. Almost anything is better than nothing, just so long as you keep doing. Often we have to treat ourselves the way you might someone who has just taken an overdose of sleeping pills. Short of pumping out his stomach, what you do is to open the windows wide, lift him by the armpits and keep walking him around the room. It's equally important that we drive ourselves in the same way. We all too easily settle for planning and putting off, promising and putting off, proposing and putting off, while it's only *what we actually do* that's going to have a beneficial effect. Yes, even though we may, in fact, worsen our situation somewhat by having done the wrong thing—we all make mistakes—just by keeping the habit of *doing* alive, there's a good chance we'll eventually develop the good habit of *doing something different*.

QUESTION: But when we work from nine to five as most of us do and have, in fact, pretty much the same tasks to perform from day to day, how can you expect us to do things differently?

ANSWER: Of course, there are limitations. I am not suggesting that we live our lives totally without rules, regulations, form, structure. Nor is it advisable that we substitute total unpredictability for predictability. Let's try to arrange life so we have *both* elements in it. Let's *add* change to the sameness, not substitute change *for* it. Instead of listening to the same news every morning that we heard the night before, let's listen to some music; it might do more for us. Eat something different for breakfast, go to work a different way. Experiment with different approaches to the tasks that await you at the office. Make friends with different people there, whom you've possibly overlooked. Do something different at lunch. Have a sandwich in and spend the hour exploring a part of town you seldom visit, or make a point of going out to lunch with someone with whom you can talk about the things you enjoy. Plan your evenings ahead of time, instead of waiting for the last moment—only to be disappointed. Go to see the dancers visiting from Thailand only because you've never seen anything like that before. You might go to the library only because you haven't been there in years. I daresay no matter how fully we may think we live life, the chances are there are more things available which we have *not* done or even tried than those which we do, in fact, enjoy. This is the way to add to the number of things we like to do. The point of it all should be clear: *change is a psychological necessity we often overlook*. Unquestionably there are demands made upon us for conformity, regularity, sameness in our behavior, and to a large degree we have no alternative but to perform from day to day in this fashion. We are not, however, totally without freedom to introduce elements of variety into our lives, the absence of which drags us down more than we realize. No doubt we have other deeper reasons for displeasure, sadness, even depression, but that is all the more reason for us to give extra special attention to those things *within our control*. We can even make a *habit* of introducing new elements into our overall experience.

Exploring new interplanetary worlds doesn't do much for us *personally*. But tasting a new food, trying a different kind of movie, making a different kind of friend, altering the order in which you do things—any of these things can help you feel somewhat more alive than you did the day before. Experiment with your own image from time to time. If you've been playing tennis like a retriever, try it like a slammer. If you've been a talker, try being a listener. If you've come on strong, try being cool and inscrutable. And finally, *one of the easiest ways of introducing elements of novelty in your life is to seek out people with enthusiasm*. They're more persuasive about trying things you haven't yet done and, being closer to their own feelings, they lead the way for you.

QUESTION: You've gotten me interested in the psychological necessities. I think what you say about change is important. What else is there?

ANSWER: *Recognition is another necessity for our sense of well-being.* I mean simply having people recognize your existence. They don't have to love you—nor should they hate you, needless to say—but merely to be aware of you and express that awareness or recognition. There is little that makes us feel more lonely than to be at a gathering where everybody, however superficially, seems to be responding to everybody else—but you. Such lack of recognition, I suspect, is even more poignant than being totally alone. When people look right past you or through you or, in general, pay no heed, you feel as if you don't belong. This, of course, amounts to rejection. A sense of unworthiness sooner or later engulfs you. It feels just awful and when it occurs often enough, you even begin to encourage people to treat you this way. Offhand, it sounds ridiculous because it's the very opposite of what you really want. But you get so used to having people look *past* you that even when they look *at* you, it's hard to believe. And so you yourself give up trying to relate to others.

QUESTION: But if you live in a large city as I do, there isn't a day of my life that I don't rub elbows with loads of people who fail to recognize me. That doesn't bother me at all. Should it?

ANSWER: No, of course not, but suppose that represented the sum total of your social experience. Suppose, with the exception of just two or three people in your life, that was it. How would you feel then?

The reasons we live as well as we do with the anonymity of city life is first, we expect it and, secondly, we have a counteragent in the friendships that we weave around us so that we are not utterly without social experience or recognition. It might even be added, because of the very thing you point out, namely, rubbing elbows daily with people who don't recognize you, that we need more of the other type of experience—awareness of others and a feeling they recognize you. You see, in the whole animal kingdom, we, as human animals, have the longest period of dependency. As a result, we are conditioned by people, to people, for people, with people—they become an indelible part of our lives and it's extremely hard to live without them. We easily lose our perspective in long periods of aloneness. Even having people in our way is more comforting than not seeing any at all. Additionally, if we spend day after day in the presence of people who obviously see us but fail to give recognition to us, we begin *to feel* as though we were nonexistent. This is because we've been programmed to live with them for so many years during our early life.

QUESTION: Okay, I can see that we need recognition from

other people, but it's still all right to pick and choose, isn't it?

ANSWER: Absolutely. Don't mistake me. I'm not talking about friendship here. I'm merely talking about recognition. If you stop at the same gas station to fill your tank again after a day or two and the attendant merely comments, "Doing a lot of driving in the last day or two, aren't you?" your reaction is not one of annoyance, why doesn't he mind his own business. On the contrary, you're rather pleased to be recognized as the same person who was in just the other day. There needn't be friendship of any significance that goes with a pleasant smile and the good-morning greeting you get from people. But when there is enough of it, you feel comfortable and unlike a total stranger. You've created a more friendly environment. It's more like being home, as compared to being lost in an unfamiliar land.

QUESTION: That last comment of yours reminds me of how I feel on many of my business trips to other cities. Although I have a sense of great freedom in not being known, I must confess I also feel somewhat uncomfortable or, at least, not so sure of myself as I am in my own territory. Is that the point you're making? Do we feel better with people we know?

ANSWER: That's exactly the point I'm making and I'm recommending that we do what we can, on a daily basis, to turn our environment into a friendly one. Not that we become lifelong friends, buddies or lovers with all the people around us. We don't have the time. There are too many things that separate us from them. But we have points of contact and that's enough to help us feel comfortable. Big-city life already has more estrangement than we need. So, get to know the newspaper man, shoeshine boy, the doorman, the local grocery store owner. Get to greet these people routinely, as well as those who work or live within reach. By giving recognition, you'll find it helps you to enjoy a sense of recognition. It isn't all that much in itself but *the absence of it* can leave you with a feeling of being cut off from others. We're hardly aware of why, yet the feeling of strangeness is there just the same.

QUESTION: Tell me more of some of the psychological necessities we tend to overlook.

ANSWER: Another extremely important one having a great deal to do with our emotional moods is *activity*. We've all become a lot more sedentary than is good for us. Many of us are simply not active enough to metabolize the food we eat; we get soft, flabby and fat after a while. Many of us are chained to our desk all day and then leave too tired to do anything about it. Our interests in sports, drama, music and the like is mostly of the spectator type so that even when we do something else in the evening, we find ourselves doing it once again in the same sedentary position. We're generally too hurried to walk anywhere, so even as we move from one place to another we do it sitting down. And the fact is *one of our basic physical* needs, one we easily overlook, *is the need* not merely for rest and relaxation, but *for activity* as well.

QUESTION: Say, maybe that's why jogging has become so popular, or bicycling on weekends.

ANSWER: No doubt about it. Every once in a while some fad appears offering people an opportunity to move, to engage in gross physical activity, and it's generally seized upon. That in itself speaks of our basic need. Once it was bowling, more recently skiing, still more recently tennis. You mentioned bicycling and jogging. The need is unquestionably enormous, but the restraining influences of city life and our jobs tend to make it, almost at best, a weekend thing.

The point is, *we are all a lot more physical than we realize.* Often, for example, we feel tired—even too tired to do anything—but what our body is inarticulately clamoring for is not rest but activity. Jogging for twenty minutes at the end of a long, self-inhibiting day might help you feel a lot better than if you were to take a forty-minute nap. Our bodily needs unfortunately don't always clarion forth clearly and exactly what they are. In the same way, we often mistake a need for temperature reduction for thirst, or hostility or boredom for hunger or, most commonly of all, boredom for fatigue. All our jobs, however interesting, still contain a great deal of sameness, which makes for boredom, and restraint, which makes for *emotional* fatigue. The popularity of bars at the end of the day expresses our need to turn it off, to reduce the poignancy of our awareness of sameness and self-containment. Working up a good sweat in some physical activity does the same job even more effectively. But once again, the crowded conditions of city life don't easily offer the opportunities for this kind of outlet. The result is that we fall out of the habit of activity very easily. Boredom and inhibition easily create sourness of mood and this makes us even more resistant to activity.

QUESTION: You said something just a little while ago I'd like to question, namely that we're often not all that aware of what our physical needs are and that they're easily confused. Is that really so?

ANSWER: Unfortunately, yes. Remember I said that often when we are bored we think we are tired, physically exhausted. What we feel as fatigue is too general an indication to have real diagnostic value. It's much like temperature. The fact that someone has a temperature of 102 doesn't mean he has a sore throat. That same elevated temperature is associated with at least a dozen other conditions requiring treatment. And so it is when we feel tired. As a matter of fact, *what we may need even more than rest is activity.* Or we may need neither rest nor activity, but rather something more interesting to do. In the same way, we often eat not when we're hungry or not even because it's eating time such as lunch or dinner. We eat because we're bored and there seems to be nothing else to do. Sometimes we eat because we're just so angry, frustrated and unhappy that any satisfaction at all develops a high priority. And food is frequently the most readily available—a mere few steps away.

QUESTION: If I may interrupt, it sounds as if there are

many times when we simply don't know what we're doing. Is that so?

ANSWER: Yes, I'm afraid there are many times when it's as simple as all that: we don't know what we're doing. People often don't realize how much they're eating or that they're heatedly yelling at someone. More of the time, we may know *what* we're doing, but *not why*. And still more often, we may know *what* we're doing and *why,* but remain unaware of the fact that it's not really going to be all that satisfying or, more important, in our best interests.

It's a mistake for us to believe that because we have a capacity for insight and consciousness, we're insightful and conscious all of the time. Sometimes it's even to our advantage not to be all that aware of what we're doing. If a person is a good driver, for example, it's very much to his advantage that he *instantaneously* do the right thing when threatened by some condition on the road, rather than have to take the time to think through what the best response would be. It might be altogether too late by then. But there are also times when this minimal awareness works against us. Sleeping—which reduces awareness to nil—is not going to get rid of boredom, for example. Nor will overeating. And precisely because it is difficult for us to make accurate determinations of what is best for us all of the time, we function better if we have well-established habits that are good for us. The man who habitually walks to work and back each day—assuming the distance is a reasonable one of a mile or so—guarantees himself a certain amount of exercise. The same is true of the woman who has a regular tennis game every Monday and Thursday evening. Eugene O'Neill's Hairy Ape used to say "T'inkin' is hard." If you have to think about it to decide whether or not to get in some tennis, the chances are you won't. The exception to this is to have strong—really strong—interests in outdoor activity. If a person truly enjoys working up a sweat, whether the activity be a hobby such as gardening or building things or sports such as bicycling, jogging or tennis, then there is a good chance that he'll use much of his free time being active. But if he enjoys it enough, he'll probably be doing these things habitually.

QUESTION: But I know lots of people who are just as happy to curl up with a good book or go to a concert or the opera. What's wrong with that?

ANSWER: There's nothing wrong with it. I'm recommending something in addition to that. True, there may be a lot of competition for our time, but if we spend all of it on the seat of our pants, our inactivity is going to show after a while. Obesity may come to plague us and the loss of tone in our bodies most certainly will. Additionally, many people suffer a vague restlessness from their inactivity. They never recognize inactivity as the origin. They just don't know that they have activity needs. Their restlessness often emits fumes of vague, ill-defined dissatisfaction and cantankerousness. In other cases, equally vague feelings of unfulfillment result in mood swings so that, without knowing why, they just feel a little blue. And most certainly what happens to most of us as a result of inactivity is a loss of sharpness; our attention declines. Many times we hear someone even say, "I've simply got to get out and walk around the block a couple of times— just to clear my head."

QUESTION: That's true. I know I've said and done that myself. But certainly you don't mean that we have to be in a constant state of motion and activity, do you?

ANSWER: Once again I must remind you that I'm suggesting something in addition to quiet and sedentary pursuits. I think it's good doctrine for us to avoid extremes in any direction. It's valuable to learn how to move, just as it is to sit still. And the same is true about other facets of our life. Ideally, we know how to talk and how to listen, how to work and how to play, how to laugh and how to cry, how to be merry and how to be serious. Balance is the important thing.

This brings me to the next of our psychological necessities

because here the question of choice and balance are extremely difficult to establish. We all dream of enjoying great serenity in our lives, but even that can be overdone. I strongly suspect that *in order to function well, we need a certain amount of excitement, tension, pressure.* A good work of art, for example, does not have its elements so totally balanced that the whole looks frozen, dead, without vitality. No, some things in it are almost always placed slightly off balance to create a little tension. True, there is an overall harmony and balance achieved, but the details of a really great work create excitement by the imbalance of some of its parts. Our lives require this too. It's a need we easily overlook, first in our dreams and then, among those old enough to retire, in the subsequent dullness of the life that often awaits them.

QUESTION: I think I know what you mean. In sports, for example, although it's important to avoid getting uptight, at critical moments in a match it's equally important not to be so relaxed that you don't put forth your best effort. But I could see that it would be hard to arrange just the right amount of each of these components in life. Do you have any suggestions along these lines?

ANSWER: What works best, I believe, is to keep trying new things and, secondly, always to strive for more. The second item needs qualification because the notion of "more" for some people has no limits. I use the word here in a sense of making a genuine effort to shoot a better round of golf or play a better game of tennis or paint a better oil. But when it's over, you recognize that your self-image or status is not dependent upon that performance. After all, you are not a pro and some ordinary performance on your part does not injure your physical, psychological or financial condition. The rest of your life will not be a shambles as a result. One of the great delights of avocational interests is that we can reach for the stars without damaging the rest of our lives if our grasp remains far short of them. It's not at all like putting your last dollar into a business venture that fails.

QUESTION: But I know people who have difficulty doing that. They play at sports with the same intensity with which they live the rest of their lives. I guess you would say that's too much excitement, tension or pressure, wouldn't you?

ANSWER: I most certainly would. They miss the point entirely when they play as hard at a game as they do at life. The whole point of the game is to have enough elements of excitement and tension to involve them, but enough that's so *unimportant* that their failure won't matter or hurt. After all, unless you're a professional golfer, why should your life be dependent upon whether or not the ball rolls into a tiny hole? Sure, you'd like it to, because that's what you're trying to do, but if it doesn't work, it doesn't really matter.

We may play hard and earnestly, but not with such dead seriousness that we don't give ourselves—and even on occasion, our opponent—a second chance. We call this gentlemanly, but actually it's a lot more. It's mature, well-adjusted and good-humored. In a game, we applaud the good shot of an opponent, whereas we don't at all in a competitive business. On the other hand it's important not to play the game or, for that matter, to live life with so little concern for its outcome that we lose interest and get bored. When that happens, we lose the game and our very taste for life.

I have a sneaking suspicion that when Henry David Thoreau built his home alongside peaceful Walden Pond over 125 years ago in his search for quiet and serenity, he found more of it than he could handle. Just as a large dosage of activity is necessary for our sense of well-being, so also do we need the stimulation that some excitement and pressure bring. I grant you the important thing is to keep it all within bounds. Lots of people I know will say from time to time, "I'd like to get into a good hot discussion and argument just for the hell of it. It's exciting if nothing else." But not all of them, once they do get into a heated discussion, stay cool enough not to say things which perhaps they later regret. Others say, "Let's take a flyer and gamble on some hot tip in the market or at the racetrack." Once again, they do it for the excitement involved, but often never stop and continue to keep things more stirred up than is good for themselves or their pocketbook. There's no question but that excitement has appeal. That's why they have some of the rides they do at amusement parks.

QUESTION: But how do we keep it in hand?

ANSWER: I'm tempted to say by being reasonable, but I know we're not reasonable human beings—at least not all of the time. The best principle is the one that issued from Aristotle over two thousand years ago when he spoke of the Golden Mean. What he meant was that the extreme in any direction is often grounds for suspicion about the quality of our adjustment. If we stay well within the bounds of the extremes, that is, out of reach of them, the chances are we'll avoid lots of trouble. But I repeat that pure, unadulterated serenity is not synonymous with the good life. We need *to use* our capacities and habits in order to live life fully and, in so doing, see the problems that mushroom up around us from time to time as having a good side as well as a bad side. Often they act like that grain of sand that irritates the oyster, which then gives up a pearl.

QUESTION: You sound so convincing. The next thing you'll tell me is that I'm lucky to have the problems I do.

ANSWER: Well, you may be in fact. There's an old philosophical story about the bird who thinks aloud how much easier it would be to fly if not for the resistance of gravity. "Oh, if only I were in a vacuum, how easy it would be." Well, put the bird in a vacuum and he falls utterly, without grace, unable to fly at all. It might be that way with us. It might well be that we need some of our problems if only to keep our problem-solving abilities sharp. This brings me to the next of our unseen psychological necessities. Hold on to your seat. I think *we even need enemies!*

QUESTION: It's going to be hard for you to convince me of that. What in the world do we need enemies for?

ANSWER: My answer is not a particularly flattering one, but I believe we all patently have more unexpressed hostility buried within us than is good for us. We recognize it in others easily enough; they recognize it in us, too. Suffice it to say, it's there and, although many of us have developed fairly effective controls in our maturity, it remains hazardous to bear such an explosive charge within us. True, we get it out in various ways; in the jargon: sublimation. We knock the cover off tennis balls, "kill" the visiting team in football, baseball and basketball, work up a sweat not only in sports but in our hobbies as well. All this helps.

QUESTION: Isn't that enough?

ANSWER: Not entirely. The reason is that human nature plays tricks on us. Nobody need anger us for us to get angry. We can merely be tired at the end of the day and since there is hostility within us, there's a good chance our controls will weaken. In other words, fatigue can begin to bring hostility close to expression. We may even feel too tired to be angry—and yet get very close to popping. But it may do us some good. Instead of letting it upset our digestive system, getting it out might be helpful. At such a time, spitting out some venom about people you consider to be public enemies might do exactly that. The danger is in getting overly worked up so you bother your digestion anyway. Worse yet, you might turn on someone close to you and that's damaging to your life.

QUESTION: I think I see what you mean. Having your own private enemies list of people who are not really close to you or important to you personally would help in that regard.

ANSWER: Exactly. In fact, if you had absolutely no personal encounter with these people it would be best. If your enemies list contains political figures you've never met, it's easy enough to find others who share your sentiments. This makes it possible to express hostility and friendship simultaneously. By beating the same drum, you strengthen the bonds with the people close to you and get rid of the hostility you feel toward more remote figures. Essentially they are scapegoats. The point is, our anger will sooner or later be discharged against others or inside ourselves; either we have scapegoats or we have symptoms. By expressing our hostility toward our "enemies" we avoid the symptoms of anything ranging from indigestion to antisocial behavior with people who count in our lives.

QUESTION: Okay. You did it. Now I see that we need enemies. Are there other unseen psychological necessities?

ANSWER: There is one other I wanted to bring to your attention—something I like to call *our pleasure level.* A good doctor, in taking care of his patient, watches his blood chemistry. He knows his patient is unaware of certain of his physical needs, but the doctor is aware of how seriously his patient's behavior and feelings could be altered by severe drops in his potassium level or elevations in his blood sugar or cholesterol. In spite of the respect we have for the mysteries of the mind, our psychological side is not nearly so complex. Instead of a constant survey of dozens of elements in our bloodstream, our psychological well-being can be examined and governed much more easily. *All we've got to watch is our daily pleasure level.* And I mean something as simple as that phrase sounds. What pleasures did we have today? Did we enjoy any of our meals? Any of the people we were with? Any of the conversations we had? Did we have some laughs? Did we sip some good wine, hear some good music, read anything worthwhile, entertain ideas we enjoyed? Make plans of interest? Reminisce warmly? Make love? The French say a day without wine is a day without sunshine. There's no reason to be so exclusive. Any of the things mentioned immediately above shines just as brightly.

QUESTION: But aren't we aware of that?

ANSWER: Yes and no. We're not at all aware of it in terms of the deliberateness of effort we put into it. Sometimes I think advertising people are more aware of it than anyone else. A highly successful campaign, for a hair dye for example, underscored the idea that blondes have more fun. Immediately after the first government report linking cancer with cigarette smoking, one of the large tobacco companies actually increased sales by suggesting now is the time for pleasure. The enormity of our response to these advertisements proves the intensity of our need for pleasure.

QUESTION: But if you have neurotic difficulties, that is, emotional problems, it's hard to be fun-loving, isn't it?

ANSWER: Indeed it is, and I daresay we all have some problems, some inner conflict, perhaps even some small neurotic difficulty. This is why it's so important that we do not overlook our need for pleasure and work on it. I always say *you can't take the business of happiness too seriously.* It doesn't just come to anyone. But there is one very simple and yet huge contribution we can make to our overall state of well-being—maintain a certain level of pleasure every day! Pleasure is not something to be taken for granted. In order to achieve it, we've got to develop the same sense of anticipation, planning and organizing we employ, on a large scale, in our major projects. Let me give you some examples of what I mean. A certain portion of anybody's day, with the exception of executives as busy as the President of the United States or the mayor of a large city, contains moments, large and small, devoted to nothing we consider of great consequence. It might be the time spent getting to work and getting home. There are often periods at work when you have to wait for something. At the end of the day, many people find themselves with nothing much to do. The trick is to use these periods in a more satisfying fashion. A fascinating novel read on the way to work might be far more enjoyable than the daily newspaper—which could be read at another time. A dry sandwich at one's desk for lunch doesn't compare with a respite from the day's work by animated conversation with a friend over a somewhat more elegant repast. Thinking ahead and arranging your evenings in advance not only makes them more enjoyable but adds the pleasures of anticipation. All but very few of us have spaces in our lives. These can be filled in many small, pleasurable ways—if we plan and work at it.

QUESTION: But will all of those small things really make a difference in our lives?

ANSWER: That's exactly the point—they do. They make a huge difference. We even say it's the small things in life that shape our destinies. No doubt it is true that there's plenty in anybody's life to drag a person down. We all, at some point or another, face sickness, death, threatening social conditions, disappointments with people. But the way we keep our head above water is by developing another side to us, a counteragent, so that like an accountant's ledger we have black as well as red entries. The more little bits and pieces of pleasure and satisfaction we have each day, the better we are able to cope. The reason is that our perspective, balance, hope and good humor all feed on pleasure, not on problems. It's important for us to maintain this level of pleasure as a buffer against the inevitable difficulties in life. One of the best theories of laughter even suggests that the reason we laugh is that if we didn't, we'd cry. Some of our best comedians, like Charlie Chaplin and a host of others, have had a sad quality about them.

QUESTION: But I have to repeat what I said earlier, that when you have problems is when you're least interested in seeking out pleasure. Isn't that so?

ANSWER: Yes, it is so, unfortunately, and that is why I emphasize the need to develop pleasure-seeking as a habit—as one of our deepest and most overriding habits. When we are in the throes of some problem, our pleasure-seeking might hopefully then be automatic and not totally erased by the emotional difficulties of the moment. There is no doubt that inner tension and conflict distract us away from pleasure. In fact, one of the common consequences of emotional difficulty is to withdraw and suffer. Relationships with people are often plundered by personal problems. We're easily given to anger, hostility, hatefulness, when we're upset and suffering. But most of us are not that deeply afflicted *all of the time*. We go through some episodes of real upset, but by and large we're not that neurotic most of the time. If during those times when we feel better rather than worse, we work at maintaining our pleasure level, we tend to handle the problems we encounter with greater balance and perspective and humor. Conversely, not doing much about our pleasure level tends to make us prone to the easy magnification of our problems.

QUESTION: By pleasure you don't mean reckless self-indulgence, do you?

ANSWER: That's a neat phrase, "reckless self-indulgence," bursting with the potential for all kinds of evil. No, I don't mean that. I mean essentially the same thing I did when I spoke of our unseen need for activity. Remember I said that if we remain too sedentary from day to day we lose our muscle tone, we get to be too limp, lax, unresponsive. We lose the tingle of good spirits. When I speak of pleasure on this daily basis, I mean it in the same sense. I mean maintaining a certain emotional tone that comes from frequent smiles and laughter. After a while we begin to expect to find something amusing because we in fact see something amusing more often. The way we live life, as outlined by our entries on application forms, is no different, *but we feel different about it.* The beat, the tempo, the key in which it's written, are all brighter. You know it's been proved experimentally that we all see something as more cheerful when it is brighter, when there is literally more light on the subject. We can do the same with our lives. It's not always an electric bulb of greater wattage, but some equally small and available adjustment that does the trick. Once we're on the lookout for more pleasure, it's easy to find innumerable ways to improve our comfort, our esthetic satisfactions, the interest with which we view people. After a while it gets to be second nature. Less effort is required and the rewards continue to increase. We even attract more people and, more and more, come to feel in possession of a great talent with which to fight off the gloom a less sharpened eye more routinely sees.

5

Everybody's Got Shortcomings—How to Turn Them into Virtues

QUESTION: That sounds to me like turning base metals into gold. What else is there to do but feel a little sorry for yourself or merely suffer through a shortcoming?

ANSWER: Of course there are things to be done, either with a condition or about it. If I were to choose a motto to be engraved on my escutcheon—a guiding principle of life—it would be *make bad good.* Serendipity, the ability to find something agreeable where you least expect it, is probably the most refreshing, rewarding experience in life. As a matter of fact, you can't make life worthwhile without some of this magic. Being born with a silver spoon by itself isn't enough, nor are the right measurements, complexion, connections or anything else. And to dream of having all these things is, well, just a dream. Sure, life is easier on paper the more of these virtues you're born with, but in reality these same virtues can be negated by a single shortcoming. The life of a rich, gorgeous girl, for example, can be so burdened by her parents' agonizingly painful relationship that she, in turn, uses or rather misuses the constant attention of men to reenact the mistrust and disappointment on which she was weaned.

QUESTION: You sure make unhappiness sound easy. Is it really that way?

ANSWER: I don't feel at all glum about our prospects, but it's true there are always obstacles. If it isn't one thing, it's another. It's kind of like gravity—constant pressure—it's just there. But we don't spend our lives on our backs because of it. We move anyway; we dance and ski and skate and enjoy ourselves nonetheless. In short, what we start life with is there —an existential given. What we do with it (and about it) offers more latitude. It's here that our imagination counts. Our road to freedom and fulfillment begins with reaching beyond "reality." You see, all growth ideally involves transcending one's origins. Life would be unbearable just with our initial equipment. We must get bigger, better, stronger, wiser. And it's not just growth; we work at it, we teach and train ourselves, shape and style ourselves, change our hair, improve our swing, fix our nose, add a skill, remove a wart, and so on and so on.

QUESTION: When you put it that way, of course, I agree. But some things are harder than others, wouldn't you say?

ANSWER: Absolutely. But we also let ourselves down. There are many things that we don't do out of sheer laziness. It's easy to put things off—like the fellow who, every time he considered getting out and doing some vigorous exercise, would lie around and wait until the feeling went away. Our laziness and inaction, surprisingly enough, don't stop us from crediting ourselves for our good intentions—even though we've accomplished nothing. But often the reasons we fail to act on our shortcomings are more subtle, less visible to the awareness we have of ourselves. I refer to an odd twist in our nature we easily miss, which is how rapidly we adjust to anything and then merely repeat and reinforce it, as well as how unaware we remain of the fact that we have adjusted at all.

Let me illustrate what I mean. Take the case of a young lady who has an overly large backside and heavy thighs; she's sensitive about it much of the time and, during the summer, dreads the idea of getting out in a bathing suit. She says, "It's the bane of my existence. I just can't live with it, nothing bothers me more. I know I'll never adjust to it." The hard fact of the matter is that she *is* living with it. Nobody can question that—not even she. She *has* adjusted to it! This is less apparent because people think of adjustment as an accomplishment, as yielding satisfaction, and they're right, even though there are good, bad and indifferent kinds of adjustment.

QUESTION: Well then, how can you say that our big-bottomed friend has adjusted to her shortcoming when we hear her complain about it all the time?

ANSWER: "All the time" gives it away. That's the clue. If the behavior is repeated again and again, *then it is part of our life-style* and not, as we would like to believe, some temporary, happy deviation from it. In short, this *is* our poor, *un*happy adjustment.

QUESTION: But if it is, where's the satisfaction? What good is her complaining doing for her?

ANSWER: Now, as the great detective Hercule Poirot, would say, we are using the little grey cells—we are thinking. When we see even our complaints, our expressions of *un*happiness, *as our way of life* and then ask what we are getting out of it, we are about to solve the problem. That is the cornerstone of clinical diagnosis and treatment. The psychologist can treat a symptom only after he has determined what that symptom is doing not merely *to* but *for* his patient. For example: Pain is what a symptom does *to* a patient and brings him to the therapist; but the therapist also has to know what that same pain is doing *for* the patient. A patient's headaches or fears may be disturbing enough to drive him to therapy. But at the same time they also give him an excuse and protect him from things that bother him even more—such as the feeling that he won't go far in his job or that he doesn't have enough class socially or won't make it with women. His symptoms take him off the hook, so to speak, and make it easier for him to accept what he is afraid he might fail at.

QUESTION: Can we get back to your earlier illustration of the young woman who is sensitive about her physical appearance? What could she be running away from?

ANSWER: Well, we look into her life and find what one might expect, namely, no love interest, in fact, not even any dates. Her explanation is obvious. How could anybody be attracted to her with her shortcomings? We look deeper and find she's afraid. Not so much of men per se but of the male-female relationship. Now we know in her case that *her* physical explanation can't possibly be adequate because she also happens to be an uncommonly pretty girl. You can't help feeling that she has no men in her life because *she runs away from them,* rather than being rejected by them. Now, of course, when the therapist looked further he couldn't blame her for running away once he learned how terrified she was of something that she herself, interestingly and yet typically, had pushed out of her mind. Much earlier in her life there was a period when she'd often be awakened in the middle of the night by the loud sounds of her parents having an argument in the adjacent room. The thin wall between them spared her none of the details of her mother's anguish over her father's repeated infidelities—her tears and accusations, her pleadings, her threats, her deep unhappiness about their life together. The daughter had come to be like the young man about to be drafted some years ago to go fight the Vietnam war. How relieved he was to discover he had high blood pressure and was classified 4F. How similarly relieved she was in declaring herself 4F for the battle of the sexes.

I'm sure there is no more bitter experience in our lives than rejection and failure. They hurt us where we hurt the most, on the deeply private level of our innermost self—not the self we try to encourage the world to see. Rejection and failure are almost more than we can bear, no matter how brave or indifferent we try to appear. As a result, most of us, even more than we know, settle in advance for a good excuse—along with some token or abortive effort—rather than take the responsibility of a total commitment to get what we want. And so we build our lives on excuses. We blame our luck, we blame the selfishness of people for not appreciating us or we blame the contradictions and absurdities of life. The point is we blame—we rationalize, we justify and maybe, most of all, we complain. We do it honestly. We believe it all and, out of it, we come to feel able to live with ourselves and even enjoy the sympathy or compassion of friends. But we've given up a lot, too. We've risked less—and we've settled for less.

QUESTION: But how could you expect that young woman to adjust any differently to her problem? You yourself said that she suffered the rejection and agony her mother did. Feeling like her mother, especially because of the physical resemblance, isn't it natural for her to fear her mother's fate?

ANSWER: We all have painful memories that scare us about our future. In this respect, she's not unusual. It may be that she'll need help eventually to get over it. But there is an enormous amount she can do for herself. Incidentally, that's always true: there's always a great deal we can do for ourselves, whether it's in overcoming a shortcoming or having nothing to do with one. It's a good habit to develop because the most common garden variety of dissatisfaction or unhappiness can be enough to prompt us to behave as she did. We all tend to settle for the excuse rather than our fulfillment. It's so imperative to be able to live with ourselves that we rush to some way of justifying our state, rather than risk making it worse by rejection and failure. You know, it's like settling for a TV dinner rather than working on a recipe for something you love but feel your inexperience will ruin anyway. And we do something even worse to ourselves. Our laziness, dissatisfaction and unhappiness about parts of ourselves all conspire to prompt us even to treat characteristics as shortcomings when they may not be at all. We profess an interest in turning our shortcomings into virtues and, crazily enough, we may be doing just the opposite. The young woman who has developed the appropriate social, sexual, athletic attitudes and skills with which to enjoy life, enjoys life with or without a heavy backside and thighs. And before long she discovers that some men are put off, others find it a matter of no importance one way or the other and still other men are actually turned on by the generous size of her bottom. In other words, what we easily see as a shortcoming may not really be one or, at most, not a very serious one. It may on the contrary even be a virtue.

QUESTION: But suppose it isn't? Does that make it valid and not merely an excuse? Or suppose a shortcoming that bugs us is something we can't change, like being overly tall or overly short?

ANSWER: The fact is it's still merely *one* feature or *part* of our total appearance. If all you could say about someone is that she's very tall or very short, what would you say if she weren't either of these? Nothing? Perhaps *that's* the shortcoming and not one's size. There ought to be lots of nice things people can say about us, either at first blush or especially after getting to know us. If there aren't, we're doing, not something wrong, but many things wrong. Most of all, we've surrendered; we've given up and built our lives on a weakness. What a foundation or basis for building anything! In so doing, we've traded satisfaction in for the minor comfort of an acceptable "reason" for our dilemma.

QUESTION: It's hard to believe that people give up so easily. Aren't they aware of this themselves?

ANSWER: You might do an informative experiment for the next couple of weeks. Ask your friends what their major shortcoming is. Many, you'll find, will just kid around and say they weren't born millionaires or devastatingly beautiful.

And even that's a significant answer. Great wealth or beauty are taken for granted as the royal road to happiness. So what your friends are saying, in their flip answer, is that they haven't the means or magic to make themselves happy. But save face they must, not only in the eyes of others, but their own, too. The absence of wealth or beauty is not good enough an excuse because it's too common. We live better with ourselves by finding a "reason" for our unhappiness more individually designed and custom-tailored. In other words, the less common, the more convincing.

But back to your experiment. You're going to find that most people are fairly vague and uncertain about what their major shortcoming is. This, despite the fact that some have noses big enough to make an eagle's look insignificant. Others have bad skin, are overweight, and so forth. Some people will say they're lazy and thus fail to take advantage of opportunities that occasionally come their way. Others flatter themselves by saying they're too good, so they get taken advantage of. Virtually nobody says, "My major shortcoming is I am unloving." Instead, they say they haven't found the right person yet. Instead of "I am rejecting," they say they are lonely. Instead of "I have no perseverance," they say people don't give them a chance. For "I have no sense of humor," they say what's so funny when you're unappreciated and underpaid. For "I am uninformed," they say so many people put on airs and show off. For "I don't have enough outside interests," they say there's never enough time for anything. Instead of "I'm dull," they say people are boring.

QUESTION: You make us sound not very smart about ourselves. Is that so?

ANSWER: I think it's safe to say that virtually nobody is as smart about himself as he is with others. All our friends could benefit from our good advice. Why can't we? Why can't we give ourselves the same good advice we give others? The fact is we can, but it's not what we want. We don't want advice. Advice is concerned with what *to do* about one's plight and we already are doing something—only it's the wrong thing. We are *defending* ourselves against hurt. By *seizing* on some shortcoming as the reason why people are not interested in us, we are *withdrawing* from them. We never see the extent of our withdrawal and so we have reason to believe that things can and hopefully will happen for the better even though we are not helping. We want something different from what we have in life, but we don't want to *do* anything different to get it. We're used to what we're doing; there's comfort in it even while we fail. Our shortcomings provide "explanations," instant solace, first aid. They may be mere props, but without them, how would we survive the long difficult journey to where we really want to be? Like Hamlet, "It makes us rather bear those ills we have, than fly to others that we know not of." Sure, we want more, but to avoid frustration and failure we settle for less. Like sleeping giants, we leave our strengths unused and, more than we readily realize, we develop a lifestyle around our weaknesses.

Many of us learn to live so well, or at least so automatically, with our shortcomings that we even slip back to them after we have gotten rid of them. A woman loses forty pounds, alters her wardrobe, buys new clothes she has always dreamed of wearing, couldn't be more pleased, and yet within a few months she's letting her clothes out again and is well on her way to a return to her former size—*and self.* Another woman siliconizes her breasts so that from flat, she is now full, prominent and shapely. She loves the way her breasts look, but it takes a long time before she feels they're hers. It takes even longer—sometimes forever—for her to feel that although her chest is different, *she* is too. For the same reason, a woman who has fixed her nose dies a thousand deaths before she tells her lover about it, even if it had been done years ago. It's not that there's anything sneaky or to be ashamed of in fixing anything these days. It's just that she still feels unpretty inside and doesn't want him to see her differently, even in his mind's eye, from what she now is.

QUESTION: I believe I see what you're getting at. I think

you're saying it's not our shortcomings but our attitudes toward ourselves, right? Just fixing the shortcoming itself may
be too narrow an approach and doesn't really do the trick.
Am I with you?

ANSWER: That's it exactly. Let me give you several other
illustrations of the same. There are people who, through
Herculean effort and splendid ability, have emerged from
painful and pitiful poverty to wealth, who still feel if they are
not careful (translation: obsessed with money and stingy),
they'll go broke. I've met countless women who have needed
love and attention so desperately they were never sure of it
when they got it and even ruined many a good marriage as a
result. Ordinarily we think that needing love would make
them loving and that getting love would satisfy the need. But
psychologically, nobody is ordinary and all too often "our
appetite grows by what it feeds on." Take a woman who still
feels, in ways, as she did as a little girl vying with her sister for
Mommy's attention; in short, she's jealous. Now, she works
hard and achieves status, cachet, style—she's up there with
the best of them. Has she turned jealousy, a shortcoming,
into a virtue? I don't feel she's turned anything into anything.
There's no transformation or magic in her behavior. What
she's done is to use jealousy to motivate her efforts to achieve
social success. She still is as acutely aware of how much attention her rivals get as she was when she was a child. It's just
that she's getting more than she once counted on and this
pleases her—at the same time that she becomes more anx-
iously dependent on this attention than ever. The need or appetite hasn't been changed; it has grown by the "success" it
has generated.

QUESTION: Is there no way out? Are we hopelessly limited
by our shortcomings forever?

ANSWER: Of course not! We're constantly making better
people of ourselves as we accumulate experience, knowledge,
insight. But at the same time if we look at ourselves re-

alistically we are also like the lamb: the older it got, the more sheepish it got. We, too, become more set in our ways even while we change for the better in other ways. Everything is going on at once. Significant improvement in ourselves must accordingly require simultaneous efforts in several directions. The woman cannot *just* have her face done or fix her nose or lose weight and expect the shortcoming to be removed and turned into a virtue. The same is true of social or psychological shortcomings. The achievement of wealth, power, recognition, status—no matter how attractive these things may be—can just as easily exaggerate our shortcomings as nullify them. Remember, we're talking about shortcomings as obstacles to happiness, not success, which can easily be pleasant and distracting enough to be mistaken for the real thing.

This isn't to say one shouldn't make the physical changes medically available or that one shouldn't work toward lofty social goals. By all means, do. But even more important is to work at living. You've got to learn that you can make yourself happy with or without your shortcomings. What happens typically is that the girl with the big nose or bad skin or flat chest learns very early that it's easier to attract men without any of these shortcomings. But when she's discouraged, she develops habits of withdrawal, supported by sour-grapes ideas that most men are boors anyway. The mere cosmetic change isn't enough to heal her feelings, change her behavior and introduce new ideas, particularly when all this has become habitual. But if instead of seizing upon the shortcoming as an excuse to withdraw from life, she worked harder at living with it, her self-defeating, isolating attitudes would never have become as strong as they are. Notice I said "if she worked *harder.*" Often it isn't even necessary. A young woman could become an excellent dancer, tennis player, live wire generally with or without the physical shortcomings we're talking about. A man doesn't have to be six and a half feet tall to be a good athlete, nor does he have to look like Robert Redford to be an interesting person. By living life more fully, these people avoid the mistake of counting on a purely cosmetic change to do everything for them. Instead, they are attacking their problem on a deeper level. They may even use their shortcomings to goad them into becoming more attractive. In this way, they maintain and even strengthen their self-image. By remaining very much part of the social scene, they become ever more deft at handling people and enjoying themselves in the process so that pleasure becomes a habit and weakness becomes a remote corner of their lives rather than its cornerstone.

QUESTION: You're sure you're not putting the cart before the horse? Most people believe that if they could get rid of some special shortcoming that bothers them, their image of themselves would improve. Isn't that so?

ANSWER: No, you were right in the first place. I *am* putting the cart before the horse, only here it works. The young man born of poverty has to learn how unimportant money can be at the very time it's important to him, in other words before he has very much of it he has to learn how to enjoy it, rather than merely respect and fear it. The young woman has to learn she can be attractive and loved before she removes the physical shortcoming that she believes to be the hopeless obstacle to being attractive and loved. The jealous person must learn how to make friends, enjoy people, feel loving and loved before his success brings him notices and pictures in the newspapers. And when a person does this, he winds up being more attractive and fulfilled, happier than most. Yes, happier even than people who seem to have been born with everything. The fact is, nobody has it all. Everyone's got obstacles, problems, shortcomings. Unlike the obvious physical ones, they may lurk in the shadows of one's inner life, but they're there. What counts in the end is the special kind of alchemy or magic we employ to turn these disadvantages to good use. If we make the mistake of believing that happiness can be a reality in our lives only when and after we remove some shortcoming that bothers us, we unfortunately discover that none of us lives long enough. Either other shortcomings will bother us or the attitudes generated by the one we couldn't get rid of for years will remain largely unchanged even after we clear ourselves of the blemish itself.

QUESTION: It all sounds very convincing, but still it's a tall order. Isn't it?

ANSWER: Yes, indeed it is. But it is because it's so easy merely to cry and feel sorry for ourselves. There's a sweet, cloying quality to wallowing in despair and there are so many things around to blame. It's like trying to diet when a fully stocked refrigerator and pantry are mere steps away. But many have done it. They've successfully licked the problem of obesity. There are many short men who have developed great stature. There are women like Liza Minnelli or Barbra Streisand who are now looked upon as beautiful and sexy. Almost everywhere we can find people who have risen from obscurity to fame. Even if all these people are exceptions, they still prove it can be done. But what I am suggesting isn't nearly that difficult. You needn't become one of the high achievers of all time to get rid of some personal obstacle. In fact, if you do, it might mean you haven't at all rid yourself of it. Your continued success might remain dependent upon it. No, what I'm saying is: "Come now, stop crying, dry your eyes, stop apologizing, no more excuses, explanations." I just want you to get going and enjoy yourself. You're not in jail or the hospital—and even there, people often find a way to lighten the burden.

Unless you recapture the ability to enjoy life, you've allowed a single shortcoming to corrupt all of it. For example, if there are no men in your life, there is still a great deal to enjoy. Even if you're poor, shy, afraid, ill, out of work, misunderstood, and so forth, there are still many things to enjoy. The greatest shortcoming of all is to become a full-time professional sufferer. It just isn't sexy. It turns people off. Worse yet, you hate yourself. So keep moving. Try this and that and all kinds of things you see others doing. Do it not because you like the idea—how can you if you haven't tried it?—but because it's good for you. You'll come to enjoy many of these things after a while. You'll make friends—new friends—and your world will expand. You'll get so involved, your short-coming will occupy less of your awareness and less of your life. You'll know you must be doing something right because you'll smile more, even laugh more. Your telephone will ring more, you'll have less time for rumination, not to mention psychological books like this.

QUESTION: You mean to say it's all that easy?

ANSWER: Well, let's say it's all that simple and it could be that easy if we weren't such sticks-in-the-mud. We all tend to be given more to repetition than to change. Anything we do to keep our flexibility alive is worthwhile. Even tiny changes in our routine will help—just for the sake of doing things differently. And above all, let's not take our ability to enjoy things for granted. That may well be our greatest blindness. We're all more than a little duller and less imaginative than we think we are. Nobody's sense of humor is as good as he believes. We tend to see what's wrong more easily than what's right. These are all obstacles to our enjoyment of life. *These* are the shortcomings that make the other ones—those we more easily recognize—so difficult to bear. Besides, if we keep in mind the theme of this book—to keep moving—we simply won't allow ourselves to take refuge in our short-comings. If we just sit and think about them, we get more and more glum and descend deeper and deeper into a black, bot-tomless pit. More positively, if we encourage ourselves to be-lieve there's lots we can try and do about things—and *do it*—we find lots of other people like ourselves trying also. They too have shortcomings. But it matters less when we're togeth-er because laughter appears once again in the company of others. What is most hopeful of all is that the shortcoming itself can serve as a reminder that we're not enjoying life enough and can goad us into doing something about it.

QUESTION: Could you recapitulate, summarize this whole thing for me?

ANSWER: Any particular shortcoming does not ruin life. Only *we* can ruin life—and then characteristically we blame it on something or other. The temptation to do this is enormous and once we do, we build a life on the excuses we make. More than we realize, we orient ourselves not toward success but toward the "explanation" of our failure. People who really want to be happy and feel deserving of it, work for it. They see their shortcomings as shortcomings, obstacles certainly, but not excuses. They achieve their goals *despite* their handicaps and, in some instances, even partially *because* of them. Almost anything worthwhile takes extra effort. The handicap merely gives us somewhat more to do, but frequently signals more sharply the need to take ourselves in hand. Our shortcomings become virtues because of what they prompt us to do for ourselves—even if we bypass them completely in the process.

CHAPTER
6

Everybody Hates
Somebody—Sometime

QUESTION: That's an odd title. Do you really believe it?

ANSWER: I do indeed. You know, of course, it's a parody on an old theme song Dean Martin used for many years, "Everybody Loves Somebody, Sometime." He was warmly reminding his audience how loving we can be and are—sometime. We all know how loving *we* are. It's the other guy we question. Unfortunately, we share the same blindness about hostility—only in reverse. We recognize everybody else's anger easily enough and tend to see our own least clearly of all. A great American philosopher, George Santayana, once wrote that if we attributed to others the just passions, noble intentions, and so on that we find in ourselves, we would take a very naive view of human nature. Although this sounds cynical, I believe it's only realistic. The two, cynicism and realism, are easily confused, but I feel not at all cynical as the first one to own up to the fact that even a clock that doesn't run is right twice a day. What I mean is that even a mean, cantankerous curmudgeon can laugh and be loving at times and, on the other side of the coin, even the most gentle, loving, Christlike figure also gets upset and angry whether he

87

shows it or not—and even he explodes visibly at times.

QUESTION: That's reasonable enough and I must confess, although I don't think of myself as a mean, angry person, there are things that upset me. But some people—wow! They're just angry all the time. Why is that?

ANSWER: Forgive me for disagreeing, but I doubt that they're angry literally all the time. They may not be happy or pleasant or affable, but it's safe to say no one is angry all the time. If it seems that way to you, that too is significant. What it means is that you've probably seen that person angry enough of the time so that (a) you don't like him and (b) you define him as a mean, angry person. Once you do that, you expect him to behave that way. You look for it in much the same way that after reading the *dramatis personae* in a play, you expect the king to act like a king, the queen to act like a queen, the knave to act like a knave, and so on. Additionally, in this guarded state there's a very good chance that you do small things to elicit the very responses you expect.

QUESTION: Wait a minute. Are you telling me that I'm responsible for the anger in many of the people I know?

ANSWER: You may well be—at least, in some small part. It's not that we go about making people angry deliberately, and heaven knows there are many people who don't need our help. Yet all of us have a way of ticking other people off, without our being aware of it. We can make a well-intentioned, uncritical remark, even while we mean to be helpful, which elicits an angry response. It doesn't necessarily mean that because the response is angry the person hates us. It may come as a result of touching a subject about which he is sensitive or sufficiently unhappy so that what he in turn says, turns out to be unpleasant. For example, a man asks his son if he can afford the purchase of the new car he is contemplating buying. He means no harm, but because his son is sensitive about money or perhaps doesn't have enough in fact to buy the car easily, he turns on his father, proclaiming that he's always critical. A woman innocently tells her husband a story about some mutual friend who was recently taken advantage of and her husband, because of his own sensitivity on the subject, jumps on her for always criticizing the friend as being a patsy. In short, what I'm saying is it's all pretty tricky. We don't have to say anything angry to get an angry response from somebody. All we have to do is touch a sensitive nerve ending.

What this adds up to is that in order to understand hostility, we can't merely subscribe to the layman's notion that some people are hostile and others aren't. That's true, but it tells the smallest part of the story. True, some people are angrier than others and express it more frequently. But we're all capable of the same thing, of getting upset and blowing off steam. What gets us upset varies from one person to another. It's safe to say in general that frustrated, unhappy, unfulfilled people will get upset more easily than others, but not always. Some have learned to keep the lid on, whereas there are people who get upset easily and often, but not terribly so. Some people become maniacal when they lose their temper, whereas others, no matter how angry they feel inside, may put in evidence little more than an acerbic word or a disdainful look. The combinations and permutations are magnified still further by the relationships we have with people. Many times, we produce an angry outburst by an innocent word. It's like flipping one's finished but lighted cigarette away into what looks like an innocent puddle but turns out to be a pool of kerosene instead.

QUESTION: From the way you put it, then, I guess we all bring about angry responses from people whether we mean to or not. Is that so?

ANSWER: Exactly. Sometimes just being there, just within earshot of a person is enough. You get into a taxi and tell the driver where you want to go and within sixty seconds he's cussing out traffic conditions, the mayor, the President, maybe even the Lord himself. And in so doing, he's starting and stopping, twisting and turning from lane to lane so that you feel as if you're in an electric mixer. Say something about his driving and he jumps on you. The fact is he's actually inviting your critical comments to add fuel to the long history of abuse he feels he's suffered at the hand of man. The unfortunate thing about it is that, more often than we want to, we give up our spectator cool and then suffer the scene through as a steamy participant. The reason is that we're cut from the same cloth and what we hate in the taxi driver, we already hate in ourselves. That is, we too feel that we are sick and tired of being a patsy, being victimized by the powers that be, the conditions that stand in our way. We too have come to believe that good guys come out last. We don't like being taken advantage of and hate ourselves for allowing it. This is our sensitive nerve ending so that the ugly invitation to get angry is more than we can refuse.

QUESTION: Okay, but you still have to admit that some people are much angrier than others. How do you explain that?

ANSWER: There's no doubt at all that some people are meaner than others. Some have a shorter fuse than others and fly off the handle quite easily. We all know some people who seem always to be looking for a fight. But I'm trying to bring us, *ourselves,* into sharpest focus, rather than *them.* I feel that the only effective way to understand hostility is by recognizing it in ourselves—where it is much more difficult to see. We dismiss our own hostility as *provoked,* rather than *natural* to us. Mightn't it be the case that others are provoked, too? There are some people whose whole life, in fact whose whole history, is a provocation. Minority groups, for example, have a long history of being taken advantage of and, as they begin to gain some small freedoms, one of the first uses to which it is put is to express their anger. You see, I am not so much interested in the academic problem of whether or not anger is some inborn trait. Even assuming it is, it varies in amount from one person or one people to another. Consistent with the emphasis throughout this book, my major interest is in *what to do* about anger, *how to handle it.*

QUESTION: Okay, so tell me what to do about that cab driver.

ANSWER: I promise I will. First, I'd like to . . .

QUESTION: Even before you do, I imagine it's going to be hard to do anything about anger if, as you say, it's common, that is, universal. Isn't that so?

ANSWER: Sure it's going to be hard. It's going to be hard because it means changing our focus. Ordinarily what happens is that somebody does something to make us angry and we respond by expressing our anger. This was not our original intention but, once we feel attacked or confronted, we respond in kind. The fact that we're justified doesn't change the bottom line. Instead of getting what we want, we get upset and, more often than not, fail to accomplish our mission. Let me illustrate what I mean. For the last several weeks you've tried to get the handyman in your building to fix a leaky faucet that drips constantly all night long, making it so difficult for you to fall asleep, you're becoming a raving insomniac. The doorbell rings one morning while you are on the phone, you rush hastily to open it and, to your pleasant surprise, find the handyman to whom you say "Come on in" and rush back to the phone. He walks in and the door slams. You stop your telephone conversation and say, not very pleasantly this time, "What did you slam the door for?" He says, "I didn't slam the door." "Don't tell me you didn't slam the door, I just heard it." "Listen, mister, I'm a plumber, not a doorman." "I can imagine what kind of a plumber you are, if you can't even close the door properly." "Listen, do you want your faucet fixed or not?" "Sure I do, but did you have to slam the door?" "Mister, you know what you can do with the door and your faucet?" This time the door really is slammed, exit the handyman, enter the drip, drip, drip of the faucet. No doubt you were tired, rushed and irritable. Although the handyman himself did not slam the door, he allowed it to slam so that in a sense you were right and you found his attitude surly. But the fact is you didn't call him to do psychotherapy, to remodel his attitudes. What you wanted was for him to fix the faucet. He was about to be a hero in your life and make sleep once again possible. If you had kept your eye on target, you would not have picked up the invitation to grapple with him. You would have wanted nothing more than to have your faucet fixed, whether he was pleasant or not. "I forgot about that door. The spring's broken. You okay? The faucet's in the bathroom right next to the bedroom."

QUESTION: I see your point, but isn't that awfully difficult to do; isn't that expecting too much of us?

ANSWER: It's not really too much to expect people to keep their eye on the ball. We don't protest against such advice in connection with golf or tennis. In fact, we know it's the only way you can hit the ball properly. If we make an effort there, in sports, certainly a real effort should be made in more important areas of life. The fact that someone is surly and upsets you need not necessarily cause you to shift gears and move in a new direction. If there is something you want from a person, get it. Don't be distracted. Sure it would be generally more pleasant if the relationship itself were a nice one. But it's not the relationship you're primarily interested in. It's something *from* the relationship and that can be obtained whether it's pleasant or not. But the reason we bite is not just an old bad habit. Our feelings of adequacy, self-assuredness and status are often so weak, we easily feel attacked and get distracted away from the issue at hand. We act as if some immediate self-assertive step must be taken. But really we are not on trial before the eyes of the world. Nobody is keeping score. Additionally, self-assertiveness is not basically established by shouting the next person down. *It's getting what you* *want that counts.* That's what's on the bottom line and that's the best indication of your adequacy.

Let's return to the cab driver you wanted to know how to handle. Remember—he's getting himself all worked up, dumping his anger and now driving in a way you find very uncomfortable. Tell him so and he attacks you; agree with him and he feels justified in continuing. In short, you simply cannot alter his behavior by doing anything one way or another about his anger. But there are other aspects, parts of his makeup that you can reach. On the very first page of this chapter, I said that "even a clock that doesn't run is right twice a day." Remember? Even though our reckless cab driver harbors a lot of hostility, he may have a compassionate side also. Suppose you manufactured a little white lie, namely, you've "just left the doctor who removed several stitches from my groin and he warned me to avoid any excess motion." I daresay your telling this to your driver would have an immediate effect on his behavior—not only for your benefit but his too, not to mention others driving or walking the same streets.

No doubt there are people who flinch at unleashing such a principle, at telling a lie—albeit white. They're not totally without reason for discomfort, but it's worth noting we don't put on our Sunday best to get rid of our garbage.

QUESTION: The white lie bothers me a little, but not really —because you're right, it works. Really what you're saying is that if you can't handle the hatefulness in someone, handle something else in him. Then you don't really have to know a great deal about the origins and causes of hostility in people?

ANSWER: All you have to know is that everybody hates somebody—sometime. And that includes you and me. Secondly, you don't have to rub people the wrong way to get them upset. They have already been rubbed. That's all you need to know about the subject. The only thing to add is something relevant, not to hostility but to life itself; namely, keep your eye on what you want. Don't be distracted by your own anger.

QUESTION: I see what you mean; but isn't it harmful to keep strong emotions all bottled up inside of you?

ANSWER: We've been taught to believe that this is the way ulcers get started, and there is some truth to it. But *expressing* our distraught emotions doesn't guarantee getting *rid* of feeling them. There are just as many people with ulcers who yell and scream easily as there are those who don't express their feelings this simply. It's perfectly appropriate after all to be upset if there is something to be upset about. Expressing the upset doesn't get rid of it. Only altering the conditions causing the upset can make a real difference. Now, of course we can't always do that. There are conditions beyond our control. But we can make life a lot easier for ourselves if our primary focus is on getting what we want and only secondarily getting involved with people's meaner feelings. In a restaurant, for example, an inattentive waiter can easily get you steamed up. But if you tangle with him, whose digestion do you disturb? His or yours? He's not eating. Even if you win your argument with him, you disturb your lunch, not his. I suggest it's wiser to be extra-special nice to him in order to get your food most expeditiously. You know the old saying, that you can attract more flies with honey than with vinegar. The point is it works, or at least works more often, than a direct frontal attack. Granted you didn't look forward to this difficulty, but if it presents itself, I'd rather switch than fight. I might downshift my behavior somewhat but I keep going in the same direction and hopefully get what I want.

Of course, there are alternatives. Someone else might request a change of table so that another waiter, possibly more attentive, might be of greater service. There's even the possibility that the restaurant down the street may be less crowded. Almost anything is better than getting into an argument before you eat. The point is you want to eat, not fight.

QUESTION: Did I hear you say be extra-special nice to a waiter who is surly with you?

ANSWER: I'm aware of the fact that such a suggestion would irk most people, but that's because most people are not terribly practical. They don't keep their eye on the bottom line and we do have a tendency in our Western society to act out our macho ideals in the most superficial way. We're satisfied by rattling a saber rather than really getting what we want.

QUESTION: Once again I find you placing the burden on us, on ourselves rather than the other person. Aren't you being unsympathetic?

ANSWER: Not at all. You remember I said earlier that people don't have to be rubbed the wrong way to act nasty. I said they already have been rubbed the wrong way by many of the details of their lives. Now, this is also true for us. But it's not always in our best interest to express our hostility directly. What I mean by this is that there are countless conditions in the lives of all of us where we don't have redress or where we're actually better off swallowing hard. Say your boss is unnecessarily critical of a piece of your work. If you stand up to him, you suffer the threat of losing your job—if he's that kind of a boss. There are many things in life like that, sources of upset which generate anger and hostility. Many are so vague and general that we don't know where to strike out and so we develop surrogates or substitutes. We take it out on someone or something else. In the jargon of psychology, this is called displacement. What it means essentially is that we all have an arsenal of hostility of varying size built up within us and, just as the waiter was perhaps taking something else that bothered him out on us, so too can our own hostility be exploded. The more generally upset we are, the more easily do we flare up in response to any specific irritation—no matter how irrelevant it may be to our overall problems.

QUESTION: I can begin to see the picture now. People don't express everything that upsets them. A lot of it gets stored away, so to speak. You never quite know when some of it is going to come out. Is that it?

ANSWER: Correct. It's as though we develop waste material but unlike the way we handle it biologically, through our organs of elimination in the bathroom—all nice and neat—on a psychological level, this emotional waste material comes out anywhere and everywhere. You remember I said earlier that you needn't even make a comment that rubs someone the wrong way. Sometimes all you have to do is be there, within earshot, and the person dumps on you. This is what makes handling hostility so difficult. It almost always catches us off guard and this is why it becomes all the more important to make deeply and extremely habitual the need to keep your eye on target. Unless we learn to act constantly in our own best interest, we easily get sidetracked and get caught up with the personalities of others. There is no objection to this if it involves people we love. But altogether too often, we get emotionally involved in a highly negative way with people who really don't mean that much to us. This is unnecessary, ineffectual and wearing.

QUESTION: I see, I see, but I feel something like jet lag before I can make the transition. I need time to develop the habit of keeping my head on straight, always keeping in view what I want and is good for me.

ANSWER: Well it's nice to take things in along the way, but as Sam Levenson once said to a child he took to a museum, "If you stop to look at everything, you're never going to get to see anything." We can only do so much. Why then pick up the challenge of every insult? Why bother with the unprovoked nastiness of people? When we respond in kind, however justified we may be, we're still being dragged off course.

QUESTION: I still have difficulty with the whole idea. Isn't it a little hypocritical to be nice to someone you really dislike, someone who is angry and making you angry?

ANSWER: To me, that kind of question is the same as asking when the Metropolitan Museum of Art pays three million dollars for a painting, "Do you think it's worth spending that kind of money for something that's red?" The color alone of the painting does not catch its essence, its true value. Similarly, someone's rudeness or anger or surliness toward you is not the whole of his relationship to you. More important than his personality—in your relationship—are his function and skill. You want a service performed, so it is not hypocritical to be effective. It is helping you get one of the most important things in the world: namely, what you want. Additionally, it maintains your emotional equilibrium and even helps the person whose behavior toward you may be reprehensible. I feel this is the effective, pragmatic way to look at it.

QUESTION: Okay, I agree. Is there anything else you can tell me to do to control *my* hostility as well as the anger of *others?*

ANSWER: Yes, there is a kind of general recommendation which is highly relevant. I mentioned that a person doesn't have to be insulted to get angry. He can just be unhappy about anything at all and that's enough to make him irritable and angry. This means that one of the most effective ways we can treat our own tendencies toward hostility is to maintain the highest level of satisfaction we can from day to day in our lives. Just as it's necessary to maintain a certain vitamin or protein level in our lives, so is it necessary to maintain a level of fulfillment and satisfaction as well. The quality of our relationship with others often reveals not just what a pain in the neck people can be, but rather how unhappy *we* may be. If we were to use our anger as that kind of honest barometer of our own feelings, we would then really put it to good use. You see I'm not just saying turn the other cheek. I'm not at all suggesting that we reconcile ourselves to the evil in life and just learn how to take it. No, what I am saying is that we ought to try our best to get the things we want, but that a great deal of this can be more easily obtained by skill and deftness than by irritability. There are different ways of winning. Sometimes it's too costly. Sometimes we win an argument and lose our friends. Long-term, it's very much more in our interests to learn how to live *with* people rather than just beat them. It's only then that the emotional tone of our lives becomes pleasant. But since we can count on hostility in people, we've got to learn how to avoid a fight and almost anesthetize them into being agreeable so that we can get what we want *through* them rather than despite them.

What this means specifically is that we approach people with a smile, a kind word, an expression of interest in them— that we treat them with the dignity human beings deserve rather than as mere things, obstacles in our path or lowly serfs left over from the Middle Ages.

QUESTION: The one possible flaw I see in all this is the difficulty of acting this way in family life. Don't you agree it would take something even more than you've covered to handle that part of our lives?

ANSWER: You're certainly making a first-rate point—one which is important enough to warrant a whole chapter in itself. See Chapter 12. The thrust of it, you'll find, is going to be much the same. To handle our own and others' hostility in family life requires the same vigilant devotion to our goals as elsewhere. The difference is that it's very much more difficult. Unlike casual relationships, members of the same family get their steam up from the same central heating system. They have more in common, greater expectations and intimacy. Additionally, home is the place we let our hair down and act out what we feel with less regard for the dictates of grace and good taste. Do this often enough over the years and you wind up with some bad habits which are not easily broken.

But age and maturity often help us see that we can't win 'em all. We learn to be less rigid, more pragmatic, and become willing to celebrate a kind of peace even if it isn't victory. There is one aspect of family life which, believe it or not, makes it easier for us to handle than other situations: we know it better! Many of us eventually use this fact to sharpen our anticipation of what will take place in family meetings and we prepare ourselves with our goals in mind. The extra dividend of such an accomplishment is that it makes it easier to act this way outside the family. Anything by comparison is easier. The surface polish we get from grown-up manners can and does help us keep our cool, but the skills we can practice at home help more effectively on the outside. They even add a confidence which raises our boiling point to safer levels.

CHAPTER
7

Everybody's Afraid
of Something

QUESTION: You mean even brave, courageous people too?

ANSWER: Yes. I mean everybody. No one's exempt from fear. Everybody's literally afraid of something, at least sometime. I remember many years ago a sports car race driver came to see me who, despite his splendid racing record, felt that he could do better if he didn't hold back out of fear. I told him he was lucky to feel that way and refused to treat him. He was disappointed, but he did admit that as the speed of automobiles increased so did the number of injuries and deaths on the track. The point is that fear has a protective quality. In its most rational form, it warns us of danger and, depending upon how afraid we get, can even sharpen our attention and concentration and make more strength and energy available to ward off the danger. In this way, fear can be of help to us. It's when fear gets out of hand, when it becomes extreme, that it can immobilize us—freeze us in our tracks—or lead to a disintegration of our behavior, as in trembling and loss of coordination. In other words, there is a difference between a rational respect for danger and an over-reaction to minor threats.

QUESTION: You're not saying then that we're all cowards, are you?

ANSWER: No. I'm saying we all have fear. As the great social scientist Thomas Hobbes once put it: "Myself and fear were born twins." The word *coward* has certain moral overtones. I believe it means being unduly afraid and unable to face threats one should or is supposed to face. It means essentially ignoble fear or timidity so that you flee from dangers you are expected to face.

QUESTION: Does the phrase "Myself and fear were born twins" mean that our fears are inborn? Are they hereditary?

ANSWER: I don't believe so at all. When something occurs very widely or even universally, there is an easy tendency to say that it is inherited. But there is no hard evidence to show that the amount of fear a person has runs in family lines.

QUESTION: Well, then, how do we get this way? Why are some people more fearful than others?

ANSWER: There are many reasons for becoming fearful. The simple fact of the matter is that we are all born very young. There is little if anything we can do for ourselves. As we become increasingly aware of the universe around us, we discover much to our chagrin that we have a marked inability to cope. We need people to look after us and we need them for a long time; in fact, longer than any other members of the animal kingdom. We experience inadequacy early in our lives on a daily and constant basis. It takes us a couple of years, for example, to reach a doorknob, only to find we don't have the strength to turn it and open the door anyway. We need help. Things are constantly appearing before us which we cannot understand and which easily alarm us—even such simple things as innocent shadows and sounds. Their unfamiliarity constantly throws us off balance. We live this way for a long time, all of which makes us fear-prone.

We develop *a tendency* to become afraid and this tendency is reinforced by our daily experience so that it's always easier for the next fear to set in. On top of that, we are often punished or threatened with punishment. That happens because it takes us a long time (a) to learn the difference between being right and wrong and (b) to develop the necessary controls over our own appetites. If you repeatedly suffer the threat of punishment along with the fear of doing something wrong and being caught, you begin to feel habitually anxious, uneasy, as though the worst were going to happen. This is the fertile ground for the development of even more specific fears.

QUESTION: That makes sense, but could you tell me more about how some specific fear develops out of all this?

ANSWER: Before I do that, I'd like to make a simple distinction between anxiety and fear. I think you'll find it helpful. The big problem we have is not so much with our specific fears as with our general anxiety. Of course, there are people whom we call phobic personalities. These are the people who have certain specific fears which in some cases, can be strong enough to reduce them to helpless invalidism. For example, a person with an extreme case of agoraphobia—a fear of open places—could become totally confined to his home. Similarly, someone else suffering from an exaggerated case of claustrophobia might not be able ever to use an automobile or an elevator. Granted these are extremes, but you can see that they practically cripple a person. Fortunately, this problem is rare. What's more common to most of us is a kind of general and vague apprehensiveness, a feeling of uncertainty about the lack of stability in our lives. Anxiety is a fear not of some specific object or event, but rather it is an anticipation of something—something which *might* take place—and, as a result, it's almost always vague, general, nebulous, shadowy, haunting.

Now, closer study of the subject strongly suggests that such anxiety reflects our general state of insecurity. This, in turn, is almost never the product of some specific upsetting experience but rather of the whole long history of the small wounds our lives leave on us. These wounds could make an almost interminable list. To mention a few: the baby's fear of Mommy's wrath when he fails to eat what she expects him to, the separating effects of darkness when he has to go to bed at night, threats of punishment for not putting his toys away, the first day of school, getting lost and separated from one's parents in a department store, the clout on the head he gets from some bigger child in the schoolyard, the embarrassment he suffers when he doesn't know the answer to a question in a classroom, the dentist's drill and the doctor's needle, the arguments between his parents. These experiences are all part of the "normal" tableau of growing up.

QUESTION: I don't mean to interrupt. I can see what happens to us as children, but how come some of us survive all this better than others?

ANSWER: You know as well as I that some of us are treated better than others. We don't all suffer the same number of experiences on the dark side and, similarly, we don't all get the same amount of tender loving care to make up for them. Some children enjoy considerably more sunshine in their early lives than others. They are often praised by their parents, treated with patience and kindness and, in general, encouraged to come to believe not only in the adequacy of their parents and their home, but in their own adequacy as well. These are the ones who grow up with much less anxiety. On the other hand, there are those children who are brought up to feel that no matter what they accomplish, it is never enough. They are constantly subject to strict moral censure and discipline. They grow up feeling inadequate to the task of fulfilling the ambitions their parents set for them. They easily develop guilt over the smallest departure from such a stringent moral code.

QUESTION: You mean, then, that once they develop anxie-

ty about themselves as a result of these experiences, it's easy
for them to become fearful of almost anything else?

ANSWER: That's right. First the soil, that is, the emotional
soil, is tilled and enriched and out of it specific fears soon
arise. Early in life, during childhood, some of these fears are
perfectly ridiculous from the adult point of view. A child can
become afraid of a common housefly, for example. You'll see
him darting around the room in the summer, dodging an ordinary little fly. There is no logic to it. It's just that once he's
fear-*prone,* anything can scare him. The reason is that "the
thing we are afraid of is generally not really the thing we are
afraid of"; we're not all that sure about what's bothering us,
making us anxious and somewhat fearful; even more important, we're even too afraid to face it if we knew. But feeling
the way we do, we have to express our fear and so we find
something else to be afraid of that scares us somewhat less
than the things we're really afraid of. Now, if all that sounds
terribly complicated, it's merely a way of saying that one of
the ways that we handle our fears is by trying to bury them
from sight. We call this repression. Unfortunately, it doesn't
totally get rid of the feelings of fear and so we find a substitute fear.

QUESTION: Most of the things we're afraid of are not really
the things we're afraid of? That's heavy. I know a young
woman who is afraid of flying. You mean to say that that's
not really the thing she's afraid of, that it's something else?

ANSWER: If you say she's afraid of flying, I accept it. She is
afraid of flying. But what would that woman have done
before airplanes were used? Do you think she would have
been fear-free? I doubt it. The point I'm making is that her
specific fear emerges out of her more general anxiety. If there
weren't airplanes, there would be something else. Moreover,
there is never merely one specific fear in an individual. Anybody who is afraid of anything is afraid of other things too.
And the reason that I'm putting it all this way is once again

to get down to the treatment of fear—what we can do about it.

QUESTION: I knew you would get to that soon enough. What can we do about it?

ANSWER: Treat the anxiety, not the fear. Granted the specific fear itself is far more dramatic and commands our attention—as well as that of others—but it's the hard way around to focus in on the fear itself. Certainly it doesn't respond to pleas of logic. Suppose you explain to a person that the most dangerous way to get anywhere has been determined statistically to be none other than walking, and the second most dangerous, driving. Does this stop you from either walking or driving? And suppose with equally accurate information you point out that the four major domestic airlines in the United States reveal that over a period of twenty-five years only one ten-thousandth of one percent of all the passengers flown during that period of time got killed. Chances are the response you would get is, "I still don't like airplanes."

QUESTION: That's true. I've seen that happen with many people. Well then, what can a person do to help himself?

ANSWER: I'm glad you put it that way; what can he *do?* Two things: (1) treat his anxiety, not the fear, and (2) work on *getting rid* of the fear rather than *expressing* it. Let me explain. I said a little while ago that we get battered about a bit by life, leaving little weaknesses in us which render us unable to handle everything that comes our way. Nobody is so totally adequate and secure that he can take care of himself totally by himself. The trouble, however, is that we underestimate how much we can help ourselves. Once you injure a knee, you favor it. Having been scolded often, you're left unsure of your judgment. Having done things we knew weren't right or even just wanting to, leaves us feeling we might, ought to or will be punished.

Such experiences leave us a little anxious about what's

going to happen to us. If these feelings persist and increase over the years, they have got to get out. We have to express them. I've seen countless people who tell me about their fears and, although they earnestly express a desire to get rid of them, I can't help but feel that there are even stronger forces within them pushing them *to express* the fears rather than *to eliminate* them. When you investigate what these people have done about getting rid of their fears, you come up with nothing. They say in their own defense: "But I've been trying." "Didn't I book an appointment with the dentist, which I admit I cancelled?" "Didn't I arrange to fly to the Caribbean but something came up at the office which made me cancel the trip?" "Didn't I promise to try to drive over that bridge, but when I broke out in a cold sweat and found myself trembling I simply had to reroute my trip?" Cold-blooded as it may sound, these are all examples of having done *nothing* to get rid of their fear. On the contrary, they are all clear-cut examples of *expressing* their fear again and again, reinforcing it rather than ridding themselves of it.

QUESTION: But they did try. Wouldn't you call those genuine efforts?

ANSWER: Not really. There's a good chance a genuine effort would succeed. And it's not entirely clear that they want to succeed. Their fear is serving a function. First, it is expressing their anxiety and if they have enough anxiety, it must be expressed. Second, it serves the purpose of retribution. In a sense they are arranging to get the punishment they feel they need. Third, it leaves them feeling sorry for themselves and even invokes the compassion of others so as to complete their momentary reinstatement among the anointed ones who think better of themselves.

QUESTION: I must say you sound hard on us. Now, what would a genuine effort be?

ANSWER: I said a moment ago the effort should be made *to* *get rid* of the fear and not *to express* it. The person who cancels his flight or his dentist appointment, if he were to focus truly on getting rid of the fear, would accept the fact that he doesn't have to enjoy the flight or the dental visit. Getting there may be half the fun for people who like to fly. But *getting there* is more important than having fun for those who are afraid. You'll enjoy yourself later, when the trip or the dental visit is done.

Suppose you suffer for several hours—that's not a crime. As a matter of fact, you're committing a crime against yourself by *not* suffering through the trip. If you stop to think of it, there are many other things we do which we abhor or labor through or sweat out or struggle over. Why does the person treat the things he's afraid to do differently? Once again, I must remind you, he does this because of what he is getting out of it. True, he wants not to be afraid. I accept that, but there are also forces within him, another side of him, so to speak, which impel him to be afraid. Unless we know what a symptom not only does *to* a person but *for* him, we can neither diagnose nor treat him successfully. To help ourselves overcome our fears, even if we are not aware of what they are doing for us, we must act on them just *because* we don't want to act on them.

QUESTION: But you mentioned treating the anxiety before and here you are telling us to treat the specific fear. Have you changed your mind?

ANSWER: No, not at all. I began to answer the question about helping ourselves to get rid of fears this way precisely because this part of the answer, I've learned, is less appealing. Mind you, I believe it is nonetheless true, but the reactions of most people have taught me that this part of the answer bothers them. The result, I hope, is that they accept much more fully the second part of the answer, the part having to do with treating the anxiety. I said earlier, you remember, that our anxiety and general feelings of insecurity are an expression of the wounds of life. The worst of all of this is what they do to our feelings about ourself. Essentially, these wounds leave us feeling inadequate and dissatisfied to be us. The more you change this, the less prone to fear you become and the more easily you can act on the first suggestion above. Suffering through a trip despite your fears, for example, would be bearable if you made it up to yourself before, during and after the trip. If we made a habit of treating ourselves better, we would feel better. And when you feel better, you feel stronger too. And when you feel stronger, you hazard more that makes you proud of yourself, so you feel better and stronger and hazard more, and so on. But this has to become a habitual part of life. It is something you have to do every day in the week. Not like the books you promised you'd read or the exercises you promised you'd do or the diet you quit after one day or the letters you never finished writing. No, this has to be an everyday occurrence. And tell me, where in town can you get a better prescription? What I am essentially saying is to treat yourself well.

QUESTION: That sounds great, but mightn't the person become an irresponsible, selfish pleasure-seeker following such advice?

ANSWER: Those who do, don't really need any encouragement. On the other hand don't overestimate our capacity for pleasure. Everybody likes to think of himself as fun-loving, good-humored, given to enjoyment—only things get in the way. A woman says *if* only my husband were more understanding, or *if* only he were more enterprising and made more money, or *if* only I got a break now and then. That tiny word *if* is like an invisible magic carpet that whisks us off to a never-never land of self-deception. Unless we learn to enjoy ourselves within the confines of *our* daily reality, we're fooling ourselves. We're saying essentially we *could* be happy, but we're not. You really have to work at learning how to be happy. It's not easy. There's a lot to learn, such as how to ride with the punches, take "no" for an answer without going to pieces, to see the humor in things . . . just to mention a few.

My mention of humor reminds me of another case of our self-blindness. Everybody thinks he has a better sense of humor than others attribute to him. In much the same way, we all like to think we are more loving and understanding than we probably are. Of course, there are things which rob us of our humor, spoil our love and certainly our good times. But it's precisely because there are so many of these things that we have to build higher thresholds for annoyance, greater resiliency. The more we enjoy ourselves in small ways, the more things we do for ourselves and others which please us, the more we get to like ourselves. *This* is essentially what makes us feel more secure. Instead of living in a guarded world full of criticism and attack, we then enjoy the warmer and the more relaxed feelings of acceptance—self-acceptance and the acceptance of others. Irrational fears don't easily develop in this kind of psychological climate.

QUESTION: As I understand you, you are saying that anything that you do to make life nicer for yourself would help eliminate fears?

ANSWER: That's it exactly. People with the greatest fears are the ones, the same ones, who are the most dissatisfied with themselves and the world. People with the fewest fears are the ones who accept themselves and life the most. Therefore, it makes sense to treat fear most effectively in terms of what fear grows out of rather than the symptom itself. For many people, this happens to be a much easier thing to do anyway. The ones who insist on treating the symptom itself, that is, each of their fears, are so deeply embroiled in their own dissatisfaction that they actually *need* the fears to express it and are merely giving lip service to getting rid of them.

QUESTION: I think I see it all clearly now, but would you mind summarizing what we do to get rid of our fears?

ANSWER: Not at all. Although most people think that their fears develop from highly upsetting experiences, they must be reminded that others have had similar upsetting experiences without developing the same fears. In other words, fear is essentially an extension of our general sense of insecurity and dissatisfaction. Countless small things happen to us, knocking us off balance, leaving us anxious, or feeling that something isn't right. It's this fear-proneness out of which specific fears are made. In the normal course of events, we all have experiences that leave us feeling that life is hard and we become unsure of ourselves, of the outcome of things, of the acceptance of others, and so on. Depending upon the amount of anxiety we have, some of it becomes more specific and is then called fear, largely because of the need to get it out. It's very difficult for us to feel threatened or worried and not express it.

The need to express these disturbed feelings is so great that although we want to get rid of our fears, we actually spend more time expressing them. Of course, we say we try, but we remain the victims of forces we cannot control. Yet the fact is that each time we fail, we actually reinforce the fear itself. *We get rid of the fear best by coming to terms with the fact that we will have to suffer through the things we are afraid of doing.* Doing exactly that—alone or with the help of someone else— works for many people.

A more significant way of going about the elimination of fear is to attack its origins, that is, our general anxiety and fear-proneness. We do this best, happily enough, with the sweetest medicine known to man: pleasure seeking! The more we do to fulfill ourselves, entertain ourselves, satisfy ourselves and, as a result, come to enjoy being ourselves, the more successfully are we acting on the potential elimination of fear. The trick is to come to enjoy ourselves and others, accept ourselves and others so that they in turn find us a joy to be with. Fear will then be relegated to a small but rational part of our life.

CHAPTER
8

How to Be Assertive— Without Rubbing People the Wrong Way

QUESTION: I'm glad you're going to consider the subject of assertiveness because frankly there are many times I'm not satisfied with myself in that I feel I haven't been assertive enough. The problem is that I always think of what I might have said or done after the event, but not when it's more appropriate, in other words, when it's happening. Can you help with something like that?

ANSWER: Well, let's try. Let's get right into it. Can you give me a concrete example of what happens with you?

QUESTION: Yes. At work, there's a fellow who acts as if he were the boss. Only the other day he said to me, "That wasn't a bad job you did on that report." "What do you mean, not a bad job?" I replied. "Well, there are a couple of things I would have done differently," he said patronizingly, adding, "As a matter of fact, I made a change or two in it." I was just dumbfounded that he had the nerve to touch anything at all in my report. Before I could say anything he handed me some papers, saying, "Here's another one you ought to get started on. I know the boss man is anxious to get the results." And off he strolled, leaving me there feeling like a little schoolboy; worse yet, more like some inadequate, limp nonentity. After all, he's not my boss. He has the same kind of job I have and as a matter of fact I've even been there longer than he. Why do I let this happen to me?

ANSWER: I have a feeling when you ask that question it's more in the nature of a complaint and that actually you can answer that question yourself, can't you?

QUESTION: I can? Yes, I suppose you're right. I can. I guess I've just always been this way.

ANSWER: That's part of it. You're saying in effect that it's a long-standing habit of response which has been reinforced again and again. But, come on now, tell me more. Why do you let such things happen to you?

QUESTION: I don't know, really. I sort of freeze up. When somebody speaks to me like that I feel like a child again. Is that why?

ANSWER: Again, that's part of it. But some children are pretty rambunctious. I gather that when you feel like a child, you feel decidedly submissive.

QUESTION: Well, if you had a father—not to mention a mother—like mine, you would have been a submissive child too. Both of them never let you get a word in edgewise. They were always right; you were always wrong. If I tried to explain, I was interrupting. I'm sure they didn't mean to but they sure made me feel like nothing. And nothing I ever did was good enough. I finally got to be the kind of a person who's never sure of himself. At college, for example, I'd almost never finish an exam because I was never sure of my answers. The result, of course, was that I'd run out of time and wind up doing not nearly so well as I probably would have done, had I finished. I suppose when you're that unsure of yourself, it's easy for people to walk all over you. Isn't it?

ANSWER: I'm afraid so. You've certainly put your finger on it. In the presence of anyone who assumes an authoritarian position with you, you can't help but reenact the painful experiences of your past.

QUESTION: If they were painful why shouldn't I avoid them?

ANSWER: That's exactly what you used to do. You avoided the disapproval of your parents by not fighting back. They were too much for you, according to your own admission, and so you submitted, you surrendered to them. But you did it so much, it became habitual and now, when anybody you meet treats you in a similarly high-handed way, you switch into your automatic response system. You don't want to, you know better, but you can't help yourself.

QUESTION: I gather that what you're really saying is that you can't be brought up one way and then act another way. In my own case, I was pushed into being submissive and so I can't expect to be assertive at the same time. You're either one or the other. Isn't that so?

ANSWER: Yes, except that it isn't all that black or white. How assertive or submissive we are exists in degrees and, to complicate the matter even more, will even vary from one situation to another. Many a man in the presence of his friends sounds very assertive in recounting his sexual exploits with women, yet in the actual presence of women he turns out to be a lamb. Many people, in the safety of their own home, give the impression of great assertiveness in talking about their experiences at work, during the war, in athletics, and yet often that verbal assertiveness bears little relationship to the facts of their behavior. I daresay there are some few distinctly assertive and unassertive people at each end of the continuum; by and large our behavior varies. Sometimes we're more one way and sometimes more the other, depending largely on the situation, our mood and what part of our personality is being reached at the time.

QUESTION: I accept that, but my *lack* of assertiveness is the problem with me; I can't say that I'm ever bothered by over-assertiveness. In fact, I wonder if anybody ever is. What do you say to that?

ANSWER: You may be right in your description of yourself and I don't doubt that there are other people like you. Yet you must be reminded that overassertiveness can be a bother to other people if not to oneself. Also, by rubbing people the wrong way we easily get ourselves in trouble. Let's say, for example, that when your co-worker at the office told you he made some changes in your report, you responded with, "I'll teach you to meddle with my report," and punched him in the nose. Whether you were justified or not, there's a very good chance that you might have gotten fired. I agree that standing there dumbfounded, offering no response, is nonfunctional but, on the other hand, lashing out physically and being overly assertive can be just as damaging. Teenagers often feel that their status in their peer group depends upon this kind of macho behavior and wind up getting themselves in trouble even in situations that began quite innocently.

QUESTION: Do I detect some effort on your part to talk me out of the value of self-assertiveness?

ANSWER: Out of the extremes, yes. In fact, out of the extremes of anything in human behavior. It's virtually psychological law that the extremes are grounds for the suspicion of neurosis. But I do want you to know that if I could wave a wand and make you either a little overassertive or a little underassertive, I would certainly choose the former for you. You'd be better off. So you see, essentially I agree with you.

QUESTION: The fellow who meddled with my report is overassertive and he doesn't seem to suffer any consequences, does he?

ANSWER: If he ever needed a helping hand, I doubt you'd be first in line to offer it to him. And just as he offended you, I suspect he's done the same to others and that they too have been rubbed the wrong way. The consequences of over-assertiveness are not necessarily immediate but they do have a way of catching up with people in the long run. Mind you, it's not that I believe in some divine distribution of justice. People who push others around frequently get their comeuppance. It's as simple as all that. The point is that they don't spread goodwill. They live a hard life, constantly on the lookout for small advantages to exploit in people. Their own underlying hostility turns even their own world into an unfriendly, mean place, however successful they seem to be in it.

QUESTION: But if what you say is so, how come so many people wish they were more assertive?

ANSWER: Because at this historic moment, it happens to be the style. At one time modesty and humility were in far better taste. They've given way to an interest in looking after Number One. There are many reasons for this, most of them having to do with the growth of freedom in our society. As wealth is more equitably distributed and we all become somewhat more affluent, the former structuring of society into imposing hierarchies of people gives way to a more genuinely democratic state. We no longer rely on hereditary titles to be called "sir," to be treated with respect. Whereas at one time government maintained class distinctions, today it tries to overcome them, and money, in our world, endows status even more quickly. Additionally, our society is an immensely competitive one. Getting ahead and winning are of immense importance. They're its primary values. To be polite, pleasant, easy to get along with, are fine but seem unrelated to achievement. There was a time in our history, now virtually forgotten, when opportunity wasn't plentiful enough to feed our competitiveness—unless, as with few exceptions, we were born rich. The luxury of getting ahead was crowded out by the fight to stay alive. Today, the redistribution of wealth and opportunity encourage us to get ahead, to win. It's no longer in bad taste to make a big noise about ourselves, to be dominant, to come out on top.

QUESTION: But those people do better, don't they? They do come out on top more often, don't they?

ANSWER: Maybe. I guess so. I don't know of any statistical studies which support the contention one way or the other, but I know some low-keyed people who have done extraordinarily well, too. The question to ask is, "What do we mean by coming out on top?" If you define success exclusively in terms of your position in the corporate structure, the amount of money you have made, the attention you have brought to yourself, then I would say a certain amount of self-assertiveness is essential. It may even be to your advantage to have more self-assertiveness than is good for you. But everybody's notions of coming out on top, of being successful, are not totally the same. Money and position are certainly the conventional signs of success. Others' notions are somewhat broader and include such goals as the satisfactions and happiness derived from the quality of our relations with people.

QUESTION: Aren't you beginning to get awfully close to imposing your own values on others?

ANSWER: Not at all! If it's success in the conventional sense that you seek, I've already stated you'd be better off with somewhat more assertiveness than average in your makeup. Assertiveness may not be absolutely necessary for success, but it helps. But like the *emotional* accountant I like to think I am, I'm merely letting you know what the personal tax is going to be on your achievement. You may make money and lose friends along the way. Assertiveness easily degenerates into hostility. Your world can become a mean, angry one.

We haven't mentioned so far what people become assertive about. Ideally, it's nice to have something to crow about before we start crowing. To assert one's self just because you believe in the equality of man doesn't prove that you are anybody's equal. You can look silly, churlish, even obstreperous; worse yet, it can become habitual. This makes us less attractive at the same time that our need for response and recognition from others increases. Instead of enjoying life more, we become more easily frustrated.

QUESTION: I feel you're right because I must confess that while on the one hand I would like to be somewhat more self-assertive than I am, on the other hand I don't really like the self-assertive people I know—or at least, most of them. I'm always more impressed with someone who keeps his cool and has enough on the ball to make his impression without much fanfare. I guess that's what you had in mind when you referred to having something to be assertive about, isn't it?

ANSWER: Let me answer your question this way. It's true we live in a highly competitive, pushy world dominated by the desire to get ahead. We've been taught how important it is to learn how to stand up and be counted and not to let ourselves get pushed around. But I must remind you that we also live in a world which is dominated by a very finely engineered division of labor. Expertise is the thing these days. You've got to know something extremely well to be regarded as a hunk of manpower. For every person who gets along and does well on sheer bravado, there are thousands who get along on hard-earned skill and effort. It's all too easy, in the current emphasis on self-assertion, to overlook this fact. True, there's a kind of Machiavellian delight in the manipulation of people to one's own ends. But it's not nearly so reliable a tool in the long run.

QUESTION: I can't help but agree with you, but just the same, I would like to learn how to do something about my own lack of assertiveness. I promise to keep it in bounds as I improve—but I am anxious to improve.

ANSWER: It's interesting to note that you still own up to having the problem even though we've explained how you developed it.

QUESTION: But don't you always say that an explanation is not a cure?

ANSWER: Absolutely, so now let's get on with what we *can do* to become somewhat more assertive. There are two paths open to us; neither is easy, but one is much easier than the other. Remember, you explained to me that when your parents put you down you were left feeling, to quote you, "like nothing." This happened often enough to become generalized into a fairly damaged self-image. You grew up discouraged to believe in yourself. Changing this attitude is the harder of the two jobs. The easier and more immediately rewarding approach has to do not with altering our feelings about ourselves; it has to do with our behavior, how we act. The fact is, not everyone who acts assertively necessarily feels that way about himself.

QUESTION: You mean to say that we often do one thing and feel another, that we don't have to feel sure of ourselves in order to act that way?

ANSWER: No, we don't. It may come easier to us if we *feel* the part, but if we're interested enough in the results, we can get ourselves to do what will work.

QUESTION: I just realized that I really didn't have to ask that last question. Of course, we all do things we don't feel. There are countless times we do things because it's expected of us. Now, what you're saying is that we can also learn to do things that we expect of ourselves, isn't that so?

ANSWER: Exactly. The whole thing is basically a learning process. Some things, of course, are harder to learn than others because of the complexity of the subject matter. Other things are harder to learn because they run counter to what we have already learned. In your own case you lived in a family of generals; both your mother and father were overly self-assertive. There was no room for a third general. You were put down and learned to accept your position as a mere foot soldier, a follower. Now you want to be a general too. *If you act like one,* people will believe it even if you don't.

QUESTION: But how can I act like one if I don't feel it?

ANSWER: A moment ago you raised that question and then withdrew it, remembering that there are many times we act one way and feel another. You aren't changing your mind about it, are you?

QUESTION: But when the feelings are strong and the habits are of long standing, isn't it difficult to do that?

ANSWER: It is indeed. Remember I said there were two things we could do to improve our feelings of self-assertiveness. Neither was easy. The best I could offer was that one was less difficult than the other.

QUESTION: Okay, how do we go about it?

ANSWER: Did you ever, while listening to classical music alone at home, get carried away somewhat by it and begin to wave your arms like the conductor of the symphony orchestra? You even may have laughed at yourself at the pure make-believe of it all. In the same way, children watching baseball on television mimic the star players right down to their idiosyncratic gestures—but in so doing, they improve their own swing or delivery of the ball. Sports fans in general, at any age, do the same thing. Look at all the two-handed tennis backhands we now have following the success of Chris Evert and Jimmy Connors. Granted we don't have anything so simple as a sports event having to do with styles of self-assertiveness, we nonetheless come upon examples often enough for us to find something to study and imitate. We all know people we'd like to be like, in this respect. They are the ones to observe. More than that, they're the ones to imitate. In the privacy of our own home, we've got to practice saying those things that we hear them say. If you had a speech to make you'd practice it. Well, this is the same thing, only instead of a whole speech, we practice making the remarks we'd like to be able to make.

I'm serious about this. The fact that some people seem to come upon it naturally doesn't mean we can't develop the same quality by looking upon it as a skill to be practiced. There are musicians like the famous Paganini of the last century who had exceptionally long fingers which were apparently able to work totally independently of each other so that no piece was too difficult for him to play. On the other hand, we've had many great virtuoso violinists who have hands no different from yours or mine. They just had to work harder at developing the necessary skills. People let themselves down by making the mistake of thinking that self-assertiveness is something you either have or don't have. It's the wrong way to define it. Practicing what you'd like to have will, before long, give it to you.

QUESTION: You mean if I practice the answers I always think of *after* the event, I would be able to think of them and act on them while somebody was lording it over me?

ANSWER: I'm glad you raised that point. That is an extremely worthwhile thing to do. I mentioned observing and imitating others; what you just suggested can work just as well. Practicing will leave you with such a large fund of appropriate replies, they'll come out even if you *feel* timid and upset. If the appropriate response has been pushed up to the forefront of your consciousness, you don't have to reach as far for it and, once you hear yourself saying something that you are satisfied with, you don't remain dumbfounded and limp and inadequate.

QUESTION: Still it sounds strange to me to practice saying these things aloud even though you're alone and needn't be embarrassed. Is that absolutely necessary?

ANSWER: Yes, it is exactly what you said, *absolutely necessary*. Knowing these things in your head is not enough, just as knowing all about yourself is not enough. It's a huge step between knowing and doing. What you just said or, really, asked, proves it. You don't mind thinking up all kinds of answers but you do feel uneasy about practicing them aloud. Nobody's going to know what you know unless you put it in evidence. And unless you do, your feelings will remain unaltered. It's basically an old story. You don't lose weight through learning about the caloric value of different foods. You don't improve your golf or tennis game merely by reading books about it. The piano lessons you once took were ineffectual without practice. In the final analysis, you haven't learned the lessons we're talking about until you have turned knowledge into habit. What you know in your head is like the menu in the restaurant. You never satisfy your hunger merely by reading it. It's much the same with self-assertiveness. You'll be satisfied only by what you get yourself *to do*. Even if you were to think up the appropriate answers right on the spot, rather than after the situation, those answers can help only if they're translated into deed.

QUESTION: I see what you mean and I know you're right, but it's still a pretty tough assignment for me. I could even work on writing down all the answers, but I know that's not good enough. I know I must actually practice saying them aloud. Isn't that so?

ANSWER: That's the only way. I must remind you that even a superexpert musician who reads a new musical score and knows he can play it, doesn't stop there. He practices and rehearses the piece again and again before he goes into concert. It's sheer happenstance—a peculiar tradition—that we practice some things and not others. All I'm suggesting is that just because we don't have a tradition of practicing these things is no reason why we shouldn't. There are many short intervals of time in virtually every day of our lives which can be used to advantage in this matter. I refer to such times as when a man is shaving or a woman is doing her hair or when we walk to the subway or bus to take us to and from work or while waiting on line somewhere, etc. Generally at such times we're doing nothing other than the automatic behavior in which we're involved. Mentally we could be doing something else, something worthwhile. These are the periods of time to dream up all those situations that might be handled better by you, if you were prepared. This is the time to "write the dialogue." Then when the time comes to practice, in the privacy of your own home, you have something to practice.

Too many people have reported to me that they tried but just couldn't think of anything during the period of time they set aside for their private rehearsals. It's like having someone thrust a microphone before you with the request, "Say something." Naturally enough we become mute. On the other hand, if you were told in advance that you'd be given an opportunity shortly to say something, you'd prepare yourself. So in a sense we have to prepare ourselves to prepare ourselves and, contrary to how it sounds, this really makes the whole process a lot easier.

QUESTION: I hesitate to ask, in the light of the difficulty I've had with this way of combating my lack of self-assertiveness, but I am curious about the more difficult approach as well. Can you tell me something about that?

ANSWER: Yes, I think it's important that we get around to it, namely the subject of our self-image. It's probably the most important single determinant of our behavior. What we do and how we do it, even in our most automatic responses, is colored by this image. Let me illustrate what I mean. People routinely say "Hello, how are you?" and shake hands when they meet, don't they? Do they all do it alike? You can take that one tiny segment of our behavior and, by observing it more carefully, make a whole host of personality distinctions. In more important areas our personality shows through with even deeper coloration. Consider situations ranging from approaching one's boss for a raise to meeting one's potential parents-in-law for the first time to delivering one's first speech before a group to the shattering experience of discovering that one's spouse is having an extramarital affair. This is a mere sample of the countless trying situations wherein we come face to face with what we think we basically are. I myself feel that this does not necessarily represent what is quintessentially us. These are difficult moments, to be sure, but there are just as many easy and satisfying things we do which bear the stamp of what we are. But there's greater drama with difficulty and thus we give it more attention. Notice that these situations have a fair amount in common. They're potential put-downs; they threaten us with rejection. And rejection is hurtful in direct proportion to the weakness of our self-image.

QUESTION: That's exactly what I'd like to strengthen. How can I learn to think and feel better about myself?

ANSWER: We learn to think better of ourselves by accumulating experiences which makes us glad to be ourselves. We look with satisfaction on a job we've done well—anything from planting some daisies which blossom to performing a complicated piece of surgery which commands the respect of our colleagues and gives us the satisfaction of saving a person's life. This is the kind of experience I mean. But not all of it has to do with work. You're pleased with the photographs you took of your recent trip, you're happy about the new friends you made on it, you enjoy maintaining a bank balance which keeps you from debt; in fact, there are many small pleasures which brighten each day of life such as your passion for music, sports, movies, books and, most of all, people. Your telephone rings often, friends call to invite you to join them, they like being with you and you with them. Life is good!

Notice that I have said little just now about super-achievement. Except for the reference to the surgeon, all of the other experiences are well within the limits of our everyday accomplishments. *We don't have to be best to enjoy a good self-image. We've got to be good for a good self-image.* A person doesn't have to win the Nobel prize to think well of himself. Of couse, he needn't turn it down or limit his strivings unless it renders all but his professional life barren. The point is that *there's a huge difference between world acclaim and self-acclaim.* The number-one person in any area of endeavor no doubt enjoys the homage paid him by the multitude. But the applause he receives is for his greatness in some special talent. The rest of his life may be plagued with the same doubts about himself he had before his climb to the top.

QUESTION: You seem to be saying that learning how to enjoy myself will do more to improve my self-image than if I were to become very successful. Is that correct?

ANSWER: There's no doubt that we live in a world which urges success upon us. It's a Nietzschean society which constantly reminds us to be "that which must ever surpass itself." It's a powerful push. The anticulture flower children and drop-outs of the sixties soon lost their appeal. We've come to recognize all over again that it's not a crime against one's self to work hard, to develop skills, to reach beyond the moon. But most of the world are not high achievers. They can still be nice human beings and enjoy a good self-image. *For a good world image, success is important. For a good self-image, the enjoyment of self is important.* We've confused the two images because we've been taught to believe that status and respectability are everything and that satisfaction with self and happiness automatically follow.

This has been the subtle and impelling lesson of our culture for so long that we virtually worship status. We emulate those who have it by dressing like them, imitating their behavior and idiom, putting into evidence what we believe will command respect. Often we even spend more money and effort than is good for us. Worse yet, the more we imitate, the less aware of it and the more removed from ourselves we become. This is when assertiveness becomes overly important to us. Our need for attention supersedes our other values and needs. We begin to demand, rather than earn it. We grow painfully sensitive to the most trivial oversight of our importance and soon make it a fetish never to let anyone get away with anything.

Self-assertiveness when pushed to this degree reveals its essential flaws. Win or lose, we strain our relationships with people. Living itself becomes a strain because too much is overly important to us. Most of all we're confusing *self-assertiveness* with *self-esteem.* We expect the person who thinks well of himself to stand up and be counted when necessary. The self-assertive person feels it's almost always necessary. His militant posture is largely compensatory, growing out of a sense of inner dissatisfaction and weakness. If he felt more accepted, he wouldn't have to insist on it so aggressively. His very intensity makes his efforts self-defeating. The trick is to get what we want *and* have people think well of us. Both are important. If a choice had to be made between self-esteem and assertiveness, self-esteem is our more precious possession. It not only enables us to live contentedly with ourselves but paves the way for a less guarded and less demanding approach to others. Being more acceptable and accepted, we find it easier simply to ask for whatever we want.

QUESTION: I follow you, yet I'm not sure I see the difference between self-esteem and self-assertiveness. If they're not one and the same, they sure are close. Doesn't it all come out the same way? How does anyone see the difference in the way I act, or maybe even more important, how can I tell whether I'm being assertive or merely expressing my self-esteem?

ANSWER: If you have to ask about it, the concepts must be close in meaning and it's precisely because they are that we confuse them. You're dead right about the difficulties involved, but let me give you some clues which should help disentangle it all. Assertiveness is an overt act and as such easily identified. It's an insistent and unyielding statement of one's position. The success with which people behave this way depends only partially on whether or not they have feelings of self-esteem. Of course, there are times in life when it's distinctly in our best interests to be self-assertive. We can learn how and alter the accent of our behavior the way we can our speech. There are dozens of books available on the subject of assertiveness training. But neither our control nor the permanence of our assertiveness is possible without some improvement in our deep-down feelings about ourselves. Assertiveness is more for show. Feelings of worthwhileness are between us and ourselves. What we do for show is often important; what we do for ourselves is always important.

QUESTION: But isn't it true that what we do for show, as you put it, is really for ourselves? Doesn't it make us feel good or bad?

ANSWER: Yes, it can make us feel good or bad, but I cannot agree with you that what we do for show is really for ourselves. Sometimes it is. Often we regret our behavior with others, not because we didn't assert ourselves but because we did. We get caught up in the interaction of our personality with theirs and feel threatened, only because we've made our assertiveness sharper and more automatic than we realize. I suspect your question in part comes out of the belief that if you're assertive enough with people to get them to treat you with respect, you would then feel greater self-respect. On paper this may look good, but in actuality assertiveness also runs the risk of rubbing people the wrong way and losing respect. Even when it works it leaves us with a very special kind of self-respect, namely, "Well, I showed him. No one's going to take advantage of me." It's an angry kind of satisfaction.

QUESTION: That's true, but I still can't see how anyone can build self-respect or esteem without getting to be really good at something.

ANSWER: I can understand your thinking so because we have been taught to believe that if we excel in something, we'll feel satisfied with ourselves. But it can also work the other way around. Ask a beginning student to give you a definition of psychology or physics and he does at once. Ask an extremely advanced student or professor and you find he has difficulty. With relatively few exceptions, the best player on his college team can't stand up to the pros—and he knows it. Achievement is rarely an end in itself; it tends to give one a clearer view of what one has not yet accomplished. This is not to say that learning to do well doesn't help our self-esteem. It's merely a warning not to put all our eggs in one basket.

It's equally important for us to have realistic goals. Ideally they would be consistent with our ability and opportunities. You can't expect to be a scratch golfer playing merely one or two rounds a week. It would be an accident, against the odds, for you to marry a brilliant, handsome, wealthy man of the world if you moved in totally different circles. This suggests that our achievements not be judged on a national scale with the same scoring system for everybody. It's frankly healthier to judge for ourselves, in terms of what we are potentially and what we are in fact. This is a more modest and helpful approach. It's a way of being kinder to ourselves. Often, however, the problem is that it's not all that easy to treat ourselves with kindness.

Many of us, unfortunately, spent many years growing up, pressed by our parents to do more, to do better. The implication was that we didn't really deserve to feel satisfied because we didn't get good enough grades, we didn't brush our teeth or bathe regularly enough, we weren't neat enough with our clothes, our manners left much to be desired, we were careless with money, we used bad language, we didn't listen or get to bed on time, and so on. All this tends to stick. Time passes, we become adults and, on a conscious level, believe we are now free to live the way we want, while on an unconscious level the same long-playing record pounds out its familiar rhythms in our heart. We still feel what we do isn't good enough. We don't make enough money, enjoy enough recognition, have the car we want, the love life, the sparkle. As one might expect, all this tends to reinforce the insufficient self-esteem with which we were raised.

As adults, it behooves us to recognize that not having all we desire is not the result of some moral judgment. It isn't that we're undeserving; it's just that this is how it is, these are the givens, the facts of life, the raw material which has still only been partially shaped. Others worked on it originally, our parents mostly. Now it's our turn. We all face the need to make a break with our yesterdays, to transcend our origins, to remold ourselves "nearer the heart's desire." If it's been drummed into us that we're not so hot and therefore we lack self-esteem or self-respect, this is what has to be corrected, the image we have of ourselves and not merely the image we project in the outside world.

QUESTION: And do we do this by learning to enjoy ourselves?

ANSWER: It sounds like an awful oversimplification when you put it that way, doesn't it? Don't be misled by this kind of understatement. The fact is it's harder to learn how to enjoy life than to become reasonably accomplished at something. Most of our formal education, beginning with the three Rs, has to do with work and skills. Very little is concerned with getting along with one's self and others. It's easy to become a successful workaholic who commands the respect of others but who remains dissatisfied with himself. Anyone's life remains imbalanced and unfulfilled by achievement alone, particularly in one area. It leaves a drabness, a lack of laughter, even a feeling of personal and social ineptitude. We all like to think we have a better sense of humor than most, but the fact that we respond to a six-million-dollar movie or a zillion-dollar amusement park doesn't mean we know how to enjoy ourselves. It's the way we live from day to day, not our departures from it, that counts.

Balance and perspective are important in order to place the appropriate value on events around us. For us to avoid misinterpretation and overreaction we need—even more than intelligence and wisdom—to satisfy our many-faceted needs. When these needs are neglected, we feel vaguely bugged, bothered, upset. This easily escalates and soon we find someone to take it out on. Why? Because there are so many people around so much of the time. They're easy and available targets. But we do use our intelligence in the process and convince ourselves they're trying to take advantage of us. And fortunately, we know how to be assertive enough to prevent that.

Contrast this with someone who feels better about himself. Instead of building a whole series of reactions on a foundation of irritability and inner dissatisfaction, his behavior is more pleasure-oriented. He laughs things off, maneuvers his way out of unnecessary scuffles, charms people rather than trying to subdue them. Instead of eating his heart out, he enjoys more of what happens around him.

QUESTION: Are you saying he can do this *because* he enjoys himself? Don't you mean he enjoys himself because he can behave that way?

ANSWER: I mean both. I know we've been taught to believe what is implied in the second of your two questions. But in order to behave this way, we need enough satisfaction with life and ourselves and people to keep our perspective. The nice thing about pleasure is that once we enjoy ourselves habitually enough, it becomes self-reproducing. As I said a moment ago, our orientation is sufficiently governed by it for us to find more and more. Contrariwise, if we remain primarily focused on our deprivations, that is, on pleasures we don't have, we're easily upset by anything we anticipate as still another disappointment.

We needn't become Pollyannas in the process of trying to

find what pleases us. There are genuine irritants in any life and it's unrealistic not to call a spade a spade. What we must do is to broaden the range of our interests. It's unfortunately true for most of us that when we're not actively interested in something, we tend not to be merely at rest, but dangerously at the point of becoming irritable. Interests keep our attention alive (and off ourselves!). Additionally, they act as bridges to people and generate in us and them favorable emotions we like to share. The net result is a good effect on how we feel about ourselves.

QUESTION: And this helps us assert ourselves if we have to —without rubbing people the wrong way?

ANSWER: The more habitually we get along well with people, the better we are at it. We no longer see them as obstacles —as many people do. They're not threats, just people, and like ourselves they're complex mixtures of good and bad. What they are with us is often the result of how we strike them, what we elicit from them. But if we're bothered and unhappy, it comes through in our behavior and it's not our best foot which gets put forward. It really does help to improve our own emotional outlook in order to get the best from others.

Let's say you find yourself in a situation of some importance where someone *is* trying to take advantage of you. There's no rule in these suggestions which eliminates the possible use of whatever strong measures you deem necessary. I'm not at all recommending that you turn the other cheek. Humility can be inappropriate; charm and social skill can be inadequate. But important situations are not the rule of life; they are the exception. When we find it the other way around, the chances are it's *we* who are looking for trouble. By developing the interests and skills to help us enjoy ourselves and others more, our "confrontations" can be coolly assertive, expressing *as much respect* for the other person as firmness of our own belief. Winning or losing—the issue or the person—itself isn't a matter of life and death; no more than the fact that one dish was spoiled on a banquet table. The trick, of course, is to make life a banquet especially in terms of all the tastes and satisfactions we develop for and in ourselves. This gives us a great deal to share with others; it makes for a pleasant climate. Soon, getting along with people becomes easy—so easy you can even express strong differences of opinion without spoiling the relationship. Not only is this more grown-up than living exclusively with "birds of a feather," but the need for assertiveness becomes more remote. We expect all kinds of opinions and behavior from people and are not threatened by them. We like ourselves and others enough to believe we can get along despite them. We've developed some skill in doing just that and life is improved because we continue to try.

QUESTION: Are you saying you really don't have to be assertive to be assertive? I know that sounds funny, but I think you know what I mean, don't you?

ANSWER: I think that puts it extremely well: *You don't have to be assertive to be assertive!* We can get what we want in other ways. We needn't be militant. There's a gentler and more effective approach. But it means that we accept others as people, not as assailants. If we see life in overly competitive terms, we're too easily threatened even over trivial issues. Most of us, after all, are not professional athletes paid to win. We're not performing in a public spectacle. Life is more continuous and all-encompassing. It involves a larger cast of characters than a sporting event and places people in infinitely more complex relations with us. In sports, the compulsion to win is helpful; in life, it's ruinous. It's too angry, takes too much of our energy and loses our friends. We needn't swing that hard; our timing is more important.

The effort we put into being assertive with others is better used on ourselves—to improve our skills, to broaden our interests, to raise our self-esteem. All this helps us redefine human relationships so we see them not as intrinsically competitive but as a constant give-and-take. We win a few, we lose a few. We give and we get. In a far less threatened and angry and overworked way, we do surprisingly well.

It all reminds me of an old story about Dr. Bleuler who made important contributions to our understanding of schizophrenia. This is a major psychotic condition marked by severe emotional deterioration. The term *schizophrenic stubbornness* is commonly used to describe the virtually impenetrable mask which robs such patients of any emotional response. It seems the residents and interns of the hospital had come upon a case so extreme they felt even Dr. Bleuler would get nowhere with him. In fact, they joshed about his failure in advance while the doctor was with the patient. After half an hour the door opened and, to their dismay, doctor and patient came out arm in arm, tears streaming down the latter's face—a huge emotional reaction! "How did you do it?" they asked. The doctor replied simply, "I cried a little and he cried a little . . . and there you have it."

CHAPTER
9
Nasty Habits—Five Different Ways We Make Ourselves Miserable

QUESTION: From the title of this chapter, I gather it's all about things I *don't* want to learn. Am I right?

ANSWER: Actually you're half right. Certainly you don't want to learn different ways to make yourself miserable. But I suspect we already have some of the habits which I call nasty because of what they do to us. Worse yet, it's in the very nature of these habits for us to remain largely unaware of them. Mostly we blame others and things outside of ourselves for our misery, but we too have some unfortunate ways of contributing to our woe. This is the reason I thought we might talk about this subject. Certainly we don't want to learn or acquire these habits, but it is very much in our interest to *unlearn* them, avoid them, and the first step in that direction is to recognize them. It's imperative that we see them clearly and sharply enough to bring our fight against them out into the open.

QUESTION: I'm all for that. How shall we start?

ANSWER: Good. Let's start with some comments about the

133

nature of habit itself before we get into specifics about those habits which are making us unhappy. First of all, we must come to recognize that anything we do repeatedly can become habitual. In fact, the words *repeatedly* and *habitual* are interchangeable. This is true not only on a purely verbal level, but on a level important to human behavior.

Habits have a way of creeping up on us because so much of our behavior goes unnoticed. Often I suspect that the difficulty we have in grooving a good golf or tennis swing is the result of the casual and unnoticed way in which we practice the wrong thing. Could anyone calculate the number of times we swing a golf club or tennis racket *not at a ball,* but *casually,* in an effort merely to loosen up? We *do* loosen up, only to swing later at a ball with disastrous results. The point is all those warm-up swings add up and when we finally face the moment of truth, our swing is not the grooved one we would like to have, but rather a combination of the much-practiced sloppy one we used for our warm-up and the less practiced one for the game.

In the same way, there are some women who always look attractive, no matter what time of the day or night you stumble on them. Then there are others who are quick to tell you what they have just been through, or that they were going to do their hair last night and something happened, or how overworked they are at the office. Essentially they are aware of not looking as well as they want to; they are obviously defensive and make excuses about it. It isn't that the first group of women use some magical product advertised on television which the second group has not yet discovered. It's just that the first group of women have the habit of looking well and the second have the habit of *promising* themselves that they will.

Of course, we all have a tendency to explain away some inadequacy or bad habit in ourselves as an exception. But exceptions often repeated soon become the rule. Doing something again and again soon stamps it in as an indelible part of our life. This is why the Jesuits of old used to say that "repetition is the mother of study." And there is no area of our behavior which is not subject to this process of making something habitual. Even people who don't laugh or smile often—and attempt to explain it away by saying there was nothing to laugh or smile about—are really missing the point. The tendency to find something amusing becomes habitual with some people and the inability to find anything amusing becomes equally habitual with others. The simplest explanation is that if we don't laugh or smile often, we're not going to very easily—even in reaction to something humorous. It's in this kind of a subtle way that these habits develop and become evermore reinforced within us.

QUESTION: You mean that *not* being aware of our own habits can become a problem that should concern us?

ANSWER: Exactly! All too often we fail to see what we're doing again and again. And this is a fact almost as important as the first one I mentioned, namely that anything we do repeatedly becomes habitual. Yes, a fact of equal importance is that habits represent a part of ourselves we see *least* clearly. When a child first learns how to button his shirt, it requires every bit of his attention. As he develops this skill and uses it morning after morning, the whole process becomes so habitual as to escape his attention almost entirely. How many of you remember buttoning your shirt this morning? You see, it's part of the nature of habit to render some act automatic. It just happens, as it were.

Habitual behavior easily gets touched off by something somebody says or does. Without even thinking, we begin to respond in our habitual way. Somebody says, "I had an awful cold last week" and there are many people whose automatic response would be, "I'm just getting over one myself." "I was just parked for a light and someone ran into me the other day" generates an I-can-top-this with "Boy, that's nothing. Let me tell you what happened to me last week." Stop and examine the conversations around you, just for the fun of it, and see for yourself how habitually many people respond in this way. They don't even stop to ask, "Are you feeling better now?" or, "Were you hurt when someone ran into your car?" Instead, they immediately launch into a similar tale which they believe even more dramatic. Worse yet, after prolonging the discussion of the subject by adding their own experience, they later complain to others what a dull conversationalist so-and-so is.

These are mere minor examples of how we respond in the same way again and again. There are other things we do which, on the face of it, seem equally innocent but really do us considerable harm. I'd like to illustrate this with the first of the nasty habits I wanted to talk about, namely *the habit of complaining rather than coping.* You happen to be sitting with some friends and the subject of working conditions comes up. One of your friends begins to complain about the fact that his boss doesn't appreciate how hard he is working for him. And there may in fact be considerable legitimacy in this complaint. His comments were relevant and well taken. At first blush, this may not even be a nasty habit. However, suppose that young man tended to complain about his boss often. Stop to think of it—whenever you see him and you ask how things are going, that's what he comments on. In fact, you soon realize that he brings that subject up even when it's *not* relevant.

Now, it's a pretty safe general rule that the people who complain the *most* are the ones who do the *least* about what they are complaining about. Ask your friend and the chances are this general rule will be confirmed. If that is the case, then no matter how legitimate his complaints may be, *he is still failing to cope with the problem.* He's neither looking for another job nor finding other ways of improving his relationship with his boss. In which case, *his complaints are his adjustment.* The cold truth of the matter is that if he had worked on the conditions he's complaining about, instead of merely complaining, he mightn't have them to complain about. And so, in his case, the habit of complaining has crowded out anything worthwhile he might do about the problem.

QUESTION: And you mean he is really unaware of that, of

the fact that he is complaining rather than working on the solution of his problem?

ANSWER: Find out for yourself. The chances are that if he is doing anything at all other than complaining, it consists merely of token acts. There's a very good chance that underneath it all he might not believe that he can either improve his relationship with his boss or get a better job. He doesn't really feel able enough—think well enough of himself—to act on the belief that his life could be any better, short of being very lucky. He admits it: "Did you ever see a guy with worse luck than mine to have drawn a boss like that?" The result is that complaining is a necessary part of his life-style. The fact that his boss does not appreciate him enough gives validity to his complaints and he is willing to settle for that.

QUESTION: You mean the habit of complaining, even if justified, is a bad scene. It can make us miserable; is that what you mean?

ANSWER: That's exactly what I mean. Being right isn't enough—particularly if the condition remains uncorrected. It's like saying "I told you so" while the roof still leaks. You're getting wet even if you were right.

QUESTION: Well, then, what should he do about it? What can he do about it?

ANSWER: Uh-uh. Remember we're talking about nasty habits or ways to make ourselves miserable. This is the place to be reminded of *what not to do*. I'm willing to admit that our young friend may, in fact, be victimized by an unappreciative boss. I accept the fact that that his complaints are justified and I'm not about to say "Stop complaining," as you might tell someone else "Stop worrying." That's much too easy, pat and ineffective. But I can point out that, in joining the largest race of human beings in the world, namely, the world of breast-beaters, the dues he pays is to render himself impotent. Of course, I don't mean sexually impotent. I mean that in *not* *working with the givens* of the situation, by failing to accept bad luck as something that can be overcome by greater ingenuity and effort, he is accepting his condition as a defeat prescribed by fate. I like to believe that the *functional use of intelligence* is to *solve our problems, sharpen our ability to cope,* to *make life better for ourselves.* Unfortunately this is often superseded by a kind of esthetic, almost effete, use of our intelligence which does little more than make us sound good; we talk well, articulately, in an informed way about the facts and how impressive they are but, in stopping there, fail utterly to have a beneficial effect on our lives. In other words, we lay bare our problems, but we fail to remove them. This person's complaints have the function of making him feel victimized, martyred and, if he is convincing enough, others will cluck sympathetically over him. But the more habitual all this becomes, the less effective he is in achieving healthier goals.

QUESTION: I see what you mean, and you've got me worried. Let's get on with some of the other habits I may have that I'm not even aware of, but which have a way of spoiling things for me nonetheless. Are there any?

ANSWER: I don't mean to have the effect of worrying you, but since habits *do* have an unnoticed way of creeping up on us, an occasional hard-nosed scrutiny of ourselves might be worthwhile. Another habit many of us develop is that of *finding fault rather than finding virtue.* It's kind of a first cousin to complaining when we find fault with people and, of course, it isn't hard to do. We all have plenty of shortcomings, not to mention recurrent moods which bring the worst out in us. Only it's *not* in ourselves that we find these shortcomings that easily. Instead, we develop a special sensitivity to seeing them in others. Of all the reasons why we find fault, perhaps the most appealing is that it gives us someone to blame—someone *other* than ourselves. The need for this is so common as to make fault-finding easily habitual. At bottom, such a habit is basically that of scapegoating people. But then, from a clinical point of view, may I repeat that *"either we have* *scapegoats or we have symptoms."* No doubt our feelings of well-being are supported by scapegoating, thus allaying the blame and anguish we might otherwise suffer in ourselves— the stuff symptoms are made of.

QUESTION: Are you saying that we're critical of others because it makes it easier for us to live with ourselves?

ANSWER: Well, in a way it does. We do get ourselves off the hook. We blame others for things that go wrong. Additionally, it allows us to feel distinctly superior. We're saying, in effect, that we're smart enough *not* to have made the error and we're even perceptive enough to see who did. How many people do you know who easily admit that they are wrong, or who own up to an occasional carelessness with the truth or to a lack of fairness or to stinginess or to any of the faults they find in others? It's easy *not* to see this in ourselves because our *judgment invariably is an interpretation of the facts and not a statement of the facts themselves.* A man sees himself as prudent and others as stingy. He has the courage of his convictions whereas others are stubborn. He's spontaneous and fun-loving whereas others are irresponsible and immature. He has compassion whereas others are emotional slobs. And so it goes. . . . The behavior might be identical in ourselves and others, but the judgment we make about it can be very different.

QUESTION: But certainly there are genuine differences in the behavior of people which warrant these different interpretations, aren't there?

ANSWER: Oh, yes, of course. But in our day-to-day behavior, we rarely examine ourselves and others all that carefully or scientifically. I think it's safe to say *we allow our feelings to dominate the judgment* and one of the strongest feelings we all have is to give ourselves the edge. Everyone wants to come out smelling like a rose. And because this is habitual, it's easy to develop the habit of finding fault with others. But it isn't that we don't pay for it. Remember, I describe this as one of the ways to make ourselves miserable. Even though we give ourselves the edge, we do it at the expense of others. *There's a persistent strain of hostility in such judgment.* It's also alienating because no one else wears the halo you've endowed on yourself. Nobody's quite good enough for you. This is tantamount to feeling that you live in a disappointing world and disappointment is not the stuff out of which happiness is made. On the contrary, the person who finds fault easily tends *not* to enjoy himself overly much with people and soon gets to be the person who complains the most.

QUESTION: I agree. These are bad habits. Instead of enjoying what there is to enjoy in people, the habit of faultfinding really turns you in the wrong direction with them. Is that what you mean?

ANSWER: Exactly. It's like biting into the pit instead of the peach. *The fact is there are right and wrong, good and bad, virtues and shortcomings, in everybody.* The trick in our adjustment to others is to look for and elicit the best in people. Then we enjoy them the most. In other words, *what comes out of them,* to a large degree, *is a product of what we bring out of them.* It's like listening to two or three recordings of the same classical piece, sometimes played even by the same orchestra but, in each case, with a different conductor. One recording is positively lyrical, another ordinary and the third, dull and leaden. Obviously, one of the conductors knew how to wave his arms differently from the others. He inspired the musicians to a greater performance. This is a good habit for *us* to develop with people, whereas fault-finding is not.

QUESTION: Sold! I'm going to keep that image in mind and practice it with people. Let's get on with some other bad habits we don't easily see in ourselves. Are there any others?

ANSWER: Indeed there are. There's one very common among us which exacts a huge toll—more than we should be willing to pay for anything. I refer quite simply to *the habit of putting off rather than doing.* In a sense, this whole book is about this bad habit. I've been saying again and again that *it's only what you do that gets up on the scoreboard.* Even increasing our knowledge and understanding comes to naught unless we act on it. But many people have lost the habit of action. They think, plot, plan, dream, promise, talk about *but do little.* Of course, it's nice, very pleasant to think, plot, plan, and so forth and admittedly doing is hard. It's effortful but not necessarily, not if we've developed the *habit* of doing. There's an old saying that if you want to get something done, give it to a busy man. He's not necessarily smarter and he certainly has less time, but he keeps his motor running enough of the time so that it purrs smoothly along actually with less effort. It's when you have to crank things up to get them started that the most effort is involved. The busy man gets things done, in short, because he gets things done. He's on the move enough of the time so that getting started is no problem. Following through, even if it involves details, is just as easy too because he does it habitually. He's a very different breed of person from the one we all know—perhaps even ourselves—who earnestly promises to get started but who repeatedly puts things off. This can be just as much a habit as getting things done. One person habitually *does* things and another habitually *promises* himself that he will.

QUESTION: You make it sound as if there were two kinds of people, just as there are fat people and thin people or tall people and short people. Are there doers and procrastinators; is it as simple as all that?

ANSWER: You're right; perhaps I am making it sound a little too simple. A person can be a doer in some areas and given to procrastination in others. Some men, for example, are efficient in their office, but keep putting off mowing the lawn on weekends. I daresay we easily put off things we don't like to do, such as paying bills, writing a long-overdue letter or fixing something which keeps breaking. Putting some things off is a reality in anybody's life. But some people do it enough of the time so that it's not unfair to call them habitual putter-offers—just as there are others whom you can count on for getting things done.

QUESTION: I was about to object to calling someone a procrastinator if the only things he put off were those he didn't like to do. But, you know, some of those things have to be done whether you like them or not. It makes me wonder whether simply not liking it is enough of an excuse for not doing it. But then there are other times when we feel blocked, when we have inner difficulties with our motivation or something, isn't that so?

ANSWER: No doubt there are many good "reasons" for putting things off. Nowadays most of us are psychologically sophisticated enough to make a real case for psychological blocks. A woman, for example, puts off balancing her checkbook because she hated math when she was a schoolgirl; she was embarrassed repeatedly by her low grades in it. Another woman puts off writing that letter to an old friend because of the conflict between wanting to maintain a warm relationship and the coolness which time and distance have imparted. Very often we postpone a task because our own level of aspiration is something we know we are not likely to fulfill. What I mean simply is that we all too often want to do better than we can most of the time. And, of course, it's easy for the conflict to stymie action. But, whatever the reasons, however real and impelling they may be, there is still the factor of plain old habit. People who keep moving get something done. It's not always their best effort and it's not always completely done, but it's a lot more than mere promise.

QUESTION: But it isn't that we don't try. I can think of times when I began something again and again but felt I was getting nowhere. Either the ideas didn't come or I didn't seem to be accomplishing enough to continue. What else could I do under the circumstances?

ANSWER: You put it very well and, if you listened sharply to what you yourself said, you'll find the answer not far off. There were two phrases you used which were the clue: (1) you said you felt you were getting nowhere; and (2) that you didn't seem to be accomplishing enough to continue. Both of those statements suggest strong feelings for a fairly quick return on your effort. You are saying in effect that your effort was not immediately rewarded by a sense of accomplishment. I don't doubt the facts. Of course what you report is true, but it's equally true that many of the things we do don't bear fruit immediately. It's only after very much *more* effort in some tasks that you begin to feel that you're really getting somewhere. But this is actually the smaller part of my answer to your question.

Motivation is almost always an iffy thing. Sometimes it's strong and at other times it's weak. It's nice to have it, but it's hard to persevere if one is totally dependent on it. I suspect you know what I am about to say, namely that *habit is a far more reliable source of perseverance.* If, when you sit down to write, you write, or when you go out to garden, you garden or when you lie down to nap, you nap—if you do these things regularly, habitually, life gets to be a lot easier. The only motivation we can reliably depend on is not so much an interest in the task itself as a self-image—something you carry with you all the time—which involves a certain standard of performance; then, whether you like something you're doing or not, you do it and do it well enough not to have to burden yourself with apologies and excuses. Not everything has to be done perfectly and not even everything has to be done. You make those discriminations with a reasonable sense of confidence and find that it's cheaper in the end than feeding a sense of inadequacy.

QUESTION: You make it sound good, but it doesn't strike me as something that can be developed overnight. I'm willing to work at it, but you yourself just said that not everything has to be done. How seriously should I take the idea of developing the habit of work?

ANSWER: I suspect that I may get a little heavy-handed in my emphasis on *doing,* but I feel it's really worth it. Far too many of us allow too much of life to escape our grasp only because of our own passivity. We settle for our dreams rather than acting on even a small portion of them. I don't mean to sound hard-bitten or cynical when I say that we don't live in a world in which the things we want become ours only because of our desire for them. Earning them is part of reality, too. There's a lot of resistance and competition out there, but there are also opportunities. To materialize them, we cannot afford anything that smacks of passivity. What's more, opportunities exist not by mere discovery; we *create* them when we keep moving. But today we suffer the tendency to talk a great deal about all of this instead of actually taking advantage of it. Lots of people *seem* very active because of the sounds they're making, but that's not the ultimate criterion.

QUESTION: But isn't it true that talking about it helps? We clarify our ideas, get more interested and eventually act on it.

ANSWER: I'm afraid that's true on paper but not in reality. I myself find a whole breed of people who keep repeating themselves instead of getting on with it. They talk things to death. I grant you, there's a great sincerity in their talk, but their earnestness is not necessarily matched by down-to-earth action. No matter how enthusiastic talk may be, it doesn't really match the exhilaration that comes from getting what has to be done behind us. Equally important is the freedom to be enjoyed on the completion of a task. The more things hang over us, the more we get used to living that way. Life gets to be filled with complaints about all we have to do and excuses for not having gotten it done. We miss too much fun and satisfaction this way. It grows into a life-style fed more on failure and unhappiness than on accomplishment and satisfaction.

QUESTION: There's a strong implication in what you say

that, although we may not be total masters of our own fate, there's a great deal more that we can do for ourselves than we are apt to. Is that what you believe?

ANSWER: Very much so. Most of us are sleeping giants who fulfill only a fractional part of our potential. I feel this is true both of our capacity for work and our capacity for play. I don't believe for a moment that we have infinite opportunity or ability. But precisely for that reason, it becomes important for us to use *more* of what we have. I grant you the accident of our birth and the twists and turns of our psychological development create many obstacles for us but we add to them —merely by repeating the wrong thing again and again and again. We see the habits developing sometimes, but mostly we are not aware of the process. Our attention is more occupied with, or even usurped by, our complaints and excuses than they are with what *we* are doing or failing to do. If we try, it's not hard to hear ourselves offering the same apology or promise again and again. *This* is the point to turn from and place the emphasis on what we *do*. There's no point in discussing still another new diet, a new resolution, a new reason for your difficulty—just eat less if you want to lose weight. One drink less is worth more than the most profound explanation of your oral fixation. One hour spent on the lawn *today* is worth more than your promises for tomorrow. We reorient our attitude by emphasizing what we do. We make it important for us to count *only* our acts.

It's sort of like our attitude toward money. You can argue forever about the value of something but, in order to acquire it, nothing spells out more clearly what one has to do than the price tag. This emphasis on what we do realistically helps us get the things we want. Additionally, we enjoy a sense of satisfaction with self which comes from being able to direct and control our own behavior. Of course, it goes without saying, nobody achieves this totally. It always remains a goal rather than a total reality. There are times in the saga of one's life when it is more difficult and other times when it is easier. But the more we develop the *habit of acting* along these lines, the less effortful it becomes. We enjoy a sense of aliveness not only for our achievement but the process, the motion by which we live, is exhilarating in itself.

QUESTION: What comes to mind as you talk is that there are some days when things just seem to move along for me. I feel as if there's nothing I can't do. And I do get lots done and enjoy that sense of exhilaration you mention. But then there are other days when I just can't seem to get started. What do I do about them?

ANSWER: We all have some days like that, but some of us have too many of them. The truth of the matter is that there is no *simple* way to overcome this problem but there is a very *reliable* way of licking it over the long term. It is by developing the *habit of motion!* The trick is to become a doer by habit. Otherwise, as I indicated earlier, you're overly dependent on your own moods and motivations—and these are too unreliable. I'll never forget the advice of a highly successful novelist who once said to me, "The only writer who finishes a book is the one who has learned to write when he doesn't feel like it."

At the expense of sounding repetitious, I must remind you that the things we make habitual are not merely such obvious ones as smoking, biting our nails, being late or misplacing our keys. *Anything can become habitual.* Nondoers, for example, *habitually* use every possible excuse *not to do* what ought to be done. A small headache, a slight cold, a little fatigue, a feeling of being put upon, a feeling that the task before them is really silly or that it's overly important—any of these conditions is easily turned into the reason for delay and postponement. No doubt one can "explain" such behavior away by sophisticated references to resistance and/or inner conflict. But the simple fact remains that if it happens repeatedly, it is the *habit of yielding* to these subtle psychological forces that comes to be the strongest deterrent to getting things done.

Additionally, such "explanations" are always a little suspect because they come *after* the fact. There are many people who compensate, that is, they work even harder when they're beset by inappropriate moods, doubts about the value of the task before them or any other distraction for that matter. What are we to say then? In other words, the same conditions that some use as excuses for putting off their work encourage other people to work harder.

This reminds me of something in the lives of my own children relevant to illness as an excuse for school. When they were sick, assuming they weren't overly so and running a high fever, we would encourage them *not* to stay home, for it would be boring, self-indulgent and ultimately teach them to overreact to illness. We hoped we could help them avoid the tendency to make excuses for work. So we encouraged them to go to school, assuring them that the day would go faster and they'd mind their illness less, whereas, at other times, if they felt like taking the day off to go to a ball game or a matinee, they would enjoy our hearty approval. The fact is they did develop a wholesome disrespect for illness and the habit of getting things done without torturing themselves with such questions as "Should I?" or "Should I now?" or "Do I have to?" (I must confess we had an occasional truant officer making puzzling inquiries at our front door from time to time, but all in all it was worth it.)

QUESTION: What you're saying, then, is that although I'll still have to face those days when I can't get started, I can make long-term progress by working at turning my excuses for postponement into an extra stimulus for work. To use your phrase, I'm going to try to develop a "wholesome disrespect" for excuses. I like that. Are there any other bad habits we don't easily recognize in ourselves which help make us unhappy?

ANSWER: Another very common one is *talking far more than we listen*. We easily enough recognize how much other people talk, how they hardly ever let you get a word in edgewise, but we tend *not* to see it in ourselves. Of course, on the face of it, it sounds friendly enough to keep up a patter of conversation with friends, but it's easily overdone. All too often, without being sharply aware of it, we often act as though silence were threatening. Many people, in fact, own up to feeling uneasy when little is said. The trouble is that talking excessively neither conceals our feelings of insecurity nor gets rid of them. And we do face the danger of becoming a bore. Even a fascinating story told again and again wears thin. Worse yet is blowing one's own horn overly much. No matter what the reason, in short, for our loquaciousness, it simply does not endear us to people. It might be added that we learn little by talking and, at least, stand a fair chance of learning something from listening.

But it's not these social difficulties which concern me the most about excessive talking. You might, in fact, even carry it off well enough to get away with it. What bothers me more is that the habitual talker is all too often the habitual non-doer. This is true often enough to make us wary about developing one habit if it's going to be at the expense of the other. Precisely because we each think we're exceptions to the rule, it becomes important for us to maintain an extra-special vigil on this matter. There are many factors in our lives which easily promote the development of this bad habit of talking too much. Age is certainly one such factor, but long before that sets in, a person's elevation to a position of authority is often a tempting invitation to pontificate about anything. At this moment in our history, modesty and humility tend to be treated like symptoms of illness and the more assertive a person is, the more he gives the impression of "having gotten it all together." Notice I say the *impression*. My own feeling is that true value is rarely resident in superficial appearances or *impressions*. But it is the style today and we are encouraged to be more outspoken than ever. One thing easily leads to another and soon we not only speak too bluntly but just too much. And once we talk too much, it's all too easy for us to become so satisfied with the impression we believe we are making that we begin to feel little need to do anything more. We're selling ourselves verbally instead of proving ourselves actually.

QUESTION: I know people like that. And I also see how any one of us might even develop into such a person. But for me personally to benefit from all of this, I wonder if you could pinpoint more clearly what "talking too much" is. How can I determine when I am talking too much?

ANSWER: That's what I call a good and honest question. It would be helpful to us if we could see the bad habit in the process of developing rather than wait until it's fully developed and has to be pointed out to us by others. We don't easily take kindly to such an observation about ourselves no matter how close a person may be to us.

We talk too much when we turn a conversation into a monologue. It's as simple as all that. The trouble is we don't recognize it when we do it. But fortunately I can tell you some of the signs. After you leave a person or group, how much can you remember of what *they told you?* If there's not much that you remember, it might be that they didn't say much. *You* said it all.

Let me give you a typical example. The father of a teenager I see tells me that "last night, my son and I finally had a real, honest-to-goodness, down-to-earth, two-hour discussion." "Wonderful. Tell me what he said." I am then righteously regaled with the pious, well-intentioned, homespun wisdom of all the things the man is proud to report to me that *he said* to his son. "But, but," I begin to interrupt, "what was Jim's response? How did he answer that question? What were his comments on this, on that, on anything and everything you said?" It soon becomes clear that there's virtually nothing the father has to report in response to my questions. He remembers nothing because there was nothing to remember. *He did all the talking.* It was a lecture, not a discussion, and this is one of the major reasons why there is no dialogue between the two of them. The only way his son could make it a conversation was to break in on the monologue and then be reprimanded for interrupting.

How often you feel interrupted is a second way of determining whether or not we talk too much. People who enjoy a conversation with others, a give-and-take, don't feel abused by interruptions nearly so much as those who usurp a conversation. A third aid in recognizing whether or not we have talked too much is to ask oneself, Did I ask many or few questions? Once again the monologists hold forth, making no end of declarative statements, but tend *not* to ask questions.

This technique can be helpful not only in solving problems with people but in any kind of social gathering. A stranger at a dinner party can wind up being your friend before the evening is over as a result of the verbal interaction you have developed. The best conversationalist is not necessarily the one who is witty or uproariously funny but the one who knows how to draw a person out. All it takes are a few questions and the willingness to listen. This kind of a display of interest in someone almost always is met with a favorable response. You come away knowing a little more and possibly with still another friend. If you did all the talking, you'd come away knowing nothing more and you might even have been bored with the person's lack of responsiveness. Only it was you who didn't give the person a chance.

QUESTION: Okay, that's helpful. You've given me very specific things to watch for in my own conversations with others. Are there any other bad habits we develop without even being aware of it which impair our life?

ANSWER: I'm sure, unfortunately, that there are many others but there is one more in particular that I would like to talk about. This is a habit common among people who have made social relationships very difficult for themselves and others. It's the *habit of responding more to the personality* of whomever they're with *than to the issue* they are discussing. Let's start by taking an exaggerated kind of this sort of thing, merely for purposes of illustration, and then we'll get on with some of the more subtle ways in which we, too, possibly foul ourselves up doing the same thing.

A person who's more than merely a little afraid of his boss, and who therefore sees him as threatening, tends not to do himself justice in the relationship with him. If the boss expresses even a small difference of opinion, he tends to interpret it as personal criticism. If the boss merely inquires about some delay, he expects to be blamed and bawled out for it. His interpretation of the facts they're sharing in their conversation is dominated by his feelings about the other person. To some degree this is justified by the nature of the relationship. You don't expect a used car salesman, for example, to tell you that the car you're looking at was in a very bad collision and has been merely patched up to look good for purposes of making a sale. There are situations, in other words, where distrust is a perfectly reasonable caveat. Then there are other times when we're too trusting—for example, when we accept a physician's opinion about a medicine he knows little more about than what the pharmaceutical company's representative recently told him.

Now, I've given these extreme examples merely to highlight the fact that what goes on between two people often depends upon what they feel about each other—even more than what they are actually doing with each other. It's like the old story about the two psychiatrists who, in passing each other in the street, greet each other with the perfectly innocent salutation, "How are you?" whereupon one of them begins to think "What does he mean by that?" He's responding not merely to the conventional greeting as such but rather to what he knows about how psychiatrists think. It should be obvious that this sort of thing gets in our way. Instead of a simple, open, warm relationship with others, we allow our likes and, unfortunately, our dislikes to dominate our reactions instead of having it the other way around. We ought to let the facts speak for themselves and then feel good or bad depending upon what they are.

QUESTION: I don't mean to trip you up but I remember your saying elsewhere that facts are often mere facets of interpretation. Wasn't it you who said that we see not merely with the eyes or hear not merely with the ears but with the heart as well?

ANSWER: You're putting me in good company. I think it was a famous French novelist who did, but certainly your point is well taken. It's much easier in scientific endeavors than it is in human relationships to see facts as they really are. I say this despite the fact that a perfectly honest physicist would own up to the difficulties he faces, even in the laboratory, with this task. But the whole thing is also a matter of degree. I did say earlier—in this very chapter, I believe—that if you like someone, you call him prudent and if you don't, you describe the same behavior as niggardly. In the same way, you call someone spontaneous and fun-loving whereas, if you think less of him, you might describe the same behavior as immature and irresponsible.

Facts really are facets of interpretation, to a large degree, particularly when we're talking about people. This can get to be bothersome. In the event we lose too much of our objectivity, our assessment of people can become utterly unrealistic. What we *feel* about people gets to be what we *fear* about them. And the more this happens, the less attentive we are to what they actually say and do. If a young woman, for example, believes that every date she has merely wants to sleep with her, she easily gets turned off—*not* by what he is or says or does but by the interpretation *she* places upon it. People often want to believe the things that support their feelings and only fairly seldom open themselves to observations which might suggest they were wrong. We may as well admit we're all biased one way or the other and, with few exceptions, it's our biases about people which limit the quality of our relationship with them.

QUESTION: Are you saying this happens all the time?

ANSWER: I really do suspect that we never look at anyone perfectly neutrally. You know, Sigmund Freud once said that the first thing you recognize about a person is whether that individual is male or female. I suppose what I'm saying is that even at the very first moment we meet anyone we don't just see another person. We have *feelings* about that person. Not necessarily strong ones, but feelings nonetheless. We feel he is important or unimportant, pleasant or unpleasant, imposing or not, stylish or not, and so on. Some people place great stock in these first impressions; others see them as too tricky to amount to much. But whether we do or not, we allow the *feeling tone* of the relationship to dominate it. And the more strongly we feel, the more easily we can be wrong.

This is exactly what happens when people fall in love—not that they are wrong all the time. But feeling wonderful or comfortable about someone doesn't necessarily mean that the relationship is going to be a good one for any length of time. Need I remind you that people can feel comfortable with each other for the wrong reasons. A man who is unhappy at home or who is getting over an unrequited love affair easily over-reacts to the smiles and "understanding" he finds in some new woman. To illustrate the point further, take the case of a woman who feels her lawyer or her dentist are right for her because they make her feel comfortable. If she is an un-assertive person easily given to feeling insecure with people, anyone who is gentle and unthreatening will make her feel comfortable—but it might also be the case that they're not competent enough to get the job done well for her.

There's hardly an area in our lives in which we aren't in-volved with people in one way or another. The relationships don't all have to be loving or highly productive but we have them, hoping they will do something for us—other than com-plicate life even more than it is already. The habit of allowing our feelings to dominate our evaluation of the relationship with these people can and does often make for difficulty.

QUESTION: I see, but just to make sure I watch for these tendencies in myself, could you repeat what those five nasty habits are?

ANSWER: Of course. First we spoke of the habit of *com-plaining rather than coping.* Secondly, there is the habit of *finding fault rather than virtue.* Third, many of us suffer the habit of *putting off rather than doing.* Fourth, we looked at the habit of *talking much more than we listen,* and finally, at the habit of *responding more to someone's personality than to the issues between us.* Hopefully, our discussion might help us see these tendencies as they exist in ourselves and, if we get worked up enough, do something about them. Contrary to this book's constant mandate to act on our problems, the thing to do about these habits is not act on them. Let them die out of disuse.

CHAPTER
10

Eat—Drink—
and Be Sexy

We no longer suffer from knowing too little about ourselves. The problem today is to use what psychology we have to good purpose and to avoid misusing and overusing it. Many people psychologize overly much. They need reminding that we're not ethereal beings unresponsive to physical conditions. We're carnate, made of flesh and blood, "ears, organs, dimensions"; our moods, thoughts and feelings are often little more than echoes of our body's reactions to the physical conditions around us.

The purpose of this chapter is to offer such a reminder. The "pleasures of the flesh" may have developed an evil connotation in our religion-influenced history, but we entertain more liberal thought on the subject today. We have a body and are physical beings. Now that we are more accepting of this condition, we cannot afford to neglect the influence our body has on us along with the direction and control we try to exert on it.

QUESTION: You really feel the body is an important influence on our psychological reactions, don't you?

ANSWER: At the extreme, there's little question of it. If you

155

have a toothache or a pinched nerve, you're going to scream and cannot be expected to murmur sweet nothings in your swain's ear. Feeling gleeful over a brisk surf and a windswept beach, you might run, jump and cry out your joy in a purely physical way. Well within these extremes, most of our reactions are more complex and involve different parts of our personality, memory and habit structure. The subtle social demands of a situation, the other people present and what parts of their personality are brought into play may be the dominant forces shaping our response. But even in this complex potpourri of influences, our body still figures more prominently than we easily recognize. Our response may in large measure be determined by such trivial physical matters as the fact that our collar is a little too tight, we ate a little too much or perhaps not enough, the room is too warm or we've been standing too long. Not only do we use our body to express what we want, but our body expresses itself as well. It tells us things and often how we feel or act is a mixture of both what we say to it and what it says to us. When motivated enough, for example, we may tell it what to do for us and push it to the point of running faster or hitting harder to win a point in a game. When we are angry and upset it actually pushes us around, making it really hard for us to keep our cool and quiet down. What we ask of our body is often the expression of prominent aspects of our personality. One man might use his body to sexualize every day in the week, another to jog ten miles a day and a third to do both. The way our body uses us depends largely on how it has been used—or unused. It's been established, for example, that sex can go on into the eighties without any special difficulty, but more often than not the elderly stop using their body for sexual purposes and, out of disuse, the body then fails to respond.

QUESTION: I'm beginning to see that there's more than initially meets the eye in the subject of the use and abuse of our bodies—isn't there?

ANSWER: Well, I think so. Mind you, not everyone takes

the same position on the issues involved. In Western society, for example, we've been largely brought up in the Roman tradition to believe that a healthy mind exists in a healthy body. More recently, Oriental teachings have begun to reach us, suggesting that we can divorce ourselves from our body by certain mental exercise. Although as a member of this world, I espouse the tradition in which we have been raised, namely the Roman one, it's not difficult to see the uses of the Oriental belief. If one were poverty-stricken and underfed or racked with pain in a hospital bed, the ability to block out messages from the body would certainly be useful. In less dramatic fashion, the reduction of physical tensions through biofeedback exercises can be useful in reducing the frequency of headaches and even in stabilizing one's blood pressure. But I think it's safe to say that the care we give our natural equipment pays off in how it functions for us. In a sense, it's no different from our automobile. If we take care of it, it runs well. We can enjoy a freedom from it. It does what we want so that we're free to enjoy the scenery.

QUESTION: Just how much care do you mean for us to give our body?

ANSWER: Before we get to that, let me touch on still another dimension of the problem before us. We have just said that if we keep our body in tune, it performs well for us. That's one aspect of the issue. Another is the appearance of our body. We live in what can be called a phenomenological world, which means that things have to be shown, be put in evidence. A millionaire commands nobody's respect if he's stingy and acts like a pauper. A beautiful woman with untidy hair, frumpy clothes and poor posture might not be seen as beautiful. Now, although we're taught that you can't tell a book by its cover, we spend billions of dollars covering things and ourselves—with everything from packaging to clothes to cosmetics. I daresay this is a substantial indication of our interest. You're initially attracted to people by how they look. Most of us, whether we act on it or not, like to look well.

When you get right down to it, our image of ourselves—our most important possession—is strongly affected by how we think we look. For this reason alone, it's important that we maintain appearances. Self-esteem is not easily nourished by a hangdog, sloppy look.

QUESTION: Aren't you really getting to the heart of the matter now? Isn't it true that if you think poorly of yourself, it's going to be extremely difficult to shape up and conceal it from the world?

ANSWER: I can't fight you on that. You're the one who's the psychologist now. But let me remind you that improving our deep-down self-image is only one way of remedying our appearance. Granted it may be the soundest, but it's also the most difficult and, for that reason, often fails. Unlike building a house where you simply have to start at the bottom, this is more like building a bridge where you can start at either end. Society helps a great deal. It sets styles and fashions and urges us to look better, even richer, than we are. We are equally encouraged to behave not as we feel but, very often, more appropriately to the situation. Thus the French say that not everyone who dances is happy. Or, a man can smile and smile and be a villain still. All of us have days when we don't feel like acting bright and cheerfully, when we don't feel like polishing ourselves up for the world, when we don't feel like being considerate, responsible, efficient. It's then that the regulating character of the social process helps keep us in line so that we put ourselves together anyway. Of course, life is a lot more effortless and satisfying when our feelings and behavior needn't fight each other, but the times are too many to count when it's the better part of wisdom *not* to act on our feelings. It's better to do what we know works for us. Most everyone, for example, feels he would like to have a sweet at the end of a meal but he also knows what it does to his waistline.

QUESTION: But that's exactly my point. I feel that the sweet wins out even if the waistline suffers. Isn't it true that people who diet do it only for a while and then regain the weight?

ANSWER: Once again you're right—at least about many people. But you must admit there are also many others who improve their self-image somewhat by losing enough weight to allow them to look admiringly at themselves in the mirror. This alone can help them for a long time. Add the additional motivation of a career—say, that of an actor or an actress—and they can stay this way most of their lives. I really do feel we can work from the inside out or from the outside in and get results either way. How successfully those results improve our self-image depends on how bad or good it is to start with. This is a suggestion consistent with the thrust of this whole book, namely that the more we do with ourselves, by ourselves, the less we need the help of doctors. Also the more useful that help will be if and when we decide to get it. On the other hand, it's often too easy a surrender which pushes people to a doctor and can handicap their efforts with him just as a defeatest attitude undermined your efforts to help yourself. In the final analysis, the doctor doesn't cure you of weight problems or any other psychological difficulties any more than the great piano teacher makes you a virtuoso. The lessons help but it's the amount of practice you do which makes the difference.

QUESTION: Okay, I'm convinced. It's important that we take good care of the physical side of our existence because our bodies will function better, look better and help with our image of ourselves. What do you recommend?

ANSWER: Well, since the word *"eat"* is the first one in the title of this chapter and we already are on the subject of maintaining our weight, perhaps we should start with that. There's no question but that the affluence of our society has brought food closer to us, has made it more available, ready for consumption, than ever before in our history. We not only have an abundance of food in the nation but huge personal stockpiles merely a few steps away from us, in our own pantry and refrigerator. Additionally, in the last ten or fifteen years, we've come to be virtually surrounded by fast-food places. If we had as many flies and mosquitos around us as we have a plenitude of food, it would feel like a plague.

The difference is, of course, that food is fun. For most people with healthy appetites, it's an all-consuming supersport. We couldn't watch baseball or football two or three times a day every day in the week. We eat not only by desire but also by habit, routine. Often when we're not eating, we talk about it. In fact, we even rave about it. Food occupies an enormous part of our environment, both physical and psychological. Our social life so often consists of "having a drink" with someone, "breaking bread" with others, attending a cocktail or dinner party or a banquet to celebrate something. The result, of course, is that it's hard not to eat too much. It's very hard. And it becomes more of a problem as our increasingly sedentary lives require less food.

Basically, it's a losing battle because our eating habits no longer bear much of a relationship to our physiological needs. We don't eat because we're hungry. We may occasionally have a pang of hunger but more often than not we eat because it's time to eat. The amount we consume also has little to do with the needs of our body. Rather, it reflects eating habits and/or the tastiness of the food before us. And even this is only part of the story. Often we eat only because we have nothing else to do. We get a little bored and restless and, since food is only a few steps away for most of us, we have a snack. Or sometimes we're upset and frustrated and, in a desperate search for some immediate satisfaction, we turn to the one that's closest to us—food. In short, we eat for many reasons but it all goes into the same place and this inevitably expands to accommodate it.

QUESTION: You make it sound almost impossible to lose weight or maintain it. Is it really that bad?

ANSWER: It's worse. What we've mentioned so far are mostly the external factors conspiring to fatten us up. What must be added to all this to make the picture more complete is the effect of our own self-image. A person who has been overweight may not like it and feel dissatisfied with his opinion of himself, but if he or she lives that way for some period of time there is an accommodation to it. *We get used to what we are even if we don't like what we are.* It's like the old saying, "There may be better places, but there's no place like home." It's comfortable. Even dissatisfaction, because of its familiarity, unfortunately becomes comfortable. This undercuts our efforts to do worthwhile things with ourselves. It's what therapists call "resistance." They find their patients want to change their life, but they don't want to do anything different about it.

Still it's very important that we do watch our weight. We've been told it's not healthy to allow ourselves to become overweight. No matter how much money we spend on our clothes, they'll never look all that good on us. We'll have to huff and puff our way through any attempts at exercise or sports and we're going to be uncomfortable sitting on anything but large modern sofas. The problem becomes more acute with age as our metabolism decreases and the quality of restaurants we frequent increases. Just as there are enough good reasons to make overeating a problem, so we have enough good reasons to work on it. This, of course, makes it a battle royal, better yet a hundred years' war. We don't win by going on a diet and losing some weight. That's a mere skirmish. The only way we make it is by incorporating the war between us and weight into our very life-style.

The word "diet" has too temporary a connotation. And by taking things away from ourselves, we're increasing our frustration and appetite. One of the basic rules about human nature is that anything we give up must be replaced—fortunately, not necessarily by the same kind of thing. Someone might be working on his stamp collection and, if he's interested enough, not at all miss the fact that he skipped dinner. If we resolve to eat less, we've got to give more of something else to ourselves. It's not easy to discover these things but it's important to learn about them—just as important as knowing the caloric value of different foods. Our devotion to food is too hard to remove, but it can be replaced. Other of our interests can come to our rescue. Instead of lunch, go shopping. Instead of dinner, make love, jog or repaint your bedroom. Some people modify their interest in food by sub-stituting quality for mere quantity. They learn that less can be more. But most important, their efforts are not intermittent, helter-skelter. It becomes part of their life-style.

Unless we are part of a breed of noneaters—traumatized by childhood experiences with food—or have an overactive thyroid, we must have the same respect for food that we have for the fire it's cooked on. It must be controlled! After a cou-ple of years of constant effort, guarding every threat of in-vasion, checking our borders routinely, the effort to maintain our weight gets somewhat easier.

The mention above of trauma in connection with food de-serves an additional note. There are people, unlike the masses who are endangered by obesity, who suffer from the extreme opposite. This is a condition known as *anorexia nervosa.* School-aged children and adults afflicted by it resemble the poverty-stricken victims of underprivileged countries. The ill-ness is still little understood and those suffering from it are strongly resistant to treatment.

QUESTION: It may sound silly to ask, but you don't suggest we start this hundred years' war, this life-style, if our weight is fine and suffers no increase, do you?

ANSWER: No, not at all. If you're lucky enough to have that kind of physiology or eating habits which don't endanger your weight, you're lucky enough not to be bothered with this problem. But it's so enormously common for us to begin to put on weight after a while that it is important to start long before the problem gets out of hand. Another worthwhile consideration in beginning to watch one's weight is to start when things in general are going fairly well for you. I realize there may be no such time in the lives of some people, but a relative judgment can be made; let us say, when things are going better rather than worse. The reason is that it's extremely difficult to take things away from yourself when you already feel that things are being taken away. Since starting is the most difficult part of the process, it's advisable to start when it's easiest for you. An upturn of one's luck is such a time. Celebrate your increase in salary with a fine but less fattening dinner. A good time to start a diet is when you fall in love. Once some regulation of food intake becomes a part of your way of life, you'll be able better to withstand the ravenous appetites created by bad luck. We must keep in mind that our craving for food often has little to do with our body. *Emotional* deprivation is a powerful source of feelings of "hunger."

QUESTION: I'm sure what you say makes sense because you don't sound as though you're anxious that we all become health nuts. It can be overdone, can't it?

ANSWER: Unless your livelihood depended upon it, as it might if you were a movie star, pushing your concern about weight to the extreme is just as narcissistic as the behavior of weight lifters who spend hours in front of a mirror flexing their muscles. Keeping oneself in good shape is not an end in itself. It's a means of coming to think well enough of oneself not to have to pay attention to oneself. It should give us freedom, not enslavement. It's the *use* of good health and a good appearance which makes it all worthwhile. Otherwise, we're like the miser who sits and repeatedly counts his money, but fails to use it for the purpose of improving his lot. It goes without saying that anything can be carried to an extreme, but the extreme always suggests the possibility of having lost sight of our real goals. No matter how temporarily satisfied with themselves they may be, I think it's safe to say that food faddists and exercise nuts fail to live the full life that they might if they put those interests in place with others.

QUESTION; I'm glad you mentioned exercise. I wanted to get on to that. Can we?

ANSWER: Before we do, there's one more comment I wanted to make about watching our weight. Obviously we watch anything by examining it periodically. We let our dentist look at our teeth a couple of times a year or a doctor look into our general condition each year. Watching our weight requires the same kind of surveillance except that it cannot be done effectively unless we examine it far more often. By that I mean at least weekly or even more often than that. If your weight changes little, the intervals can be larger, of course. Many of us fluctuate considerably from one day to the next, in which case it might even be necessary to step on a scale daily. The idea is to make it part of the same routine which involves brushing our teeth or combing our hair. The reason is twofold. First of all, many people really don't see or feel that they are getting larger and heavier unless they see it in black and white, in a number they read on a scale. Secondly, it gives us a chance to make up for the inevitable dietary indiscretions we all commit from time to time. We almost unavoidably overeat on some occasion, but we can get on a scale to see what it cost and then exercise some caution for the next day or two. It makes it much easier than to approach the gargantuan task of losing twenty or thirty pounds all at once.

The use of the body at mealtime can be a great source of pleasure. It's much like the use of some of our other sensory equipment when we enjoy the visual experience of a colorful sunset, the auditory wealth of sound at a concert, the olfactory joy of a freshly cut rose or the tactile delight of its petals against our skin. Just because eating takes place so often is no reason to allow it to become routine, unnoticed, stale. It's a good habit to be zealous about our pleasures, to refine and expand them, to modify them, to give them enough care and attention to retain the magic they have for us. This is a good use of the body, but because we can't trade it in for a new model every several years, we have to work constantly on both its use and its preservation.

Just one more brief word before we get to the subject of exercise. I don't mean to present a treatise on drinking—

which is a specific problem and off-the-track here—but a comment or two might be relevant. Everything we've said about eating is, of course, true for drinking—in fact, even more so! Anything alcoholic is at least as habit-forming as food. It's even fattening, too. Worse yet, its effects on our behavior can be more catastrophic. Still, there is a fine sociable quality to drinking which is nice to enjoy. It's enjoyed best if we keep our drinking moderate. If there is an area in life in which it is imperative that we learn how to say "no" to ourselves, this is the one. Unless we learn to stop after one or two drinks, we're headed for trouble. It's as simple as all that. And now for exercise.

Exercise, ideally, is for the purpose of limbering or loosening up and maintaining muscle tone so that we can use our body without feeling that it's fighting us. When it begins to snow, skiers begin to exercise because they haven't used certain muscles for many months and look forward to their use on the slopes once again. But people have also found that even if they don't go in for sports, they can enjoy a feeling of exhilaration and well-being on the completion of certain exercises. It's almost as though they had skied or played tennis and so the exercise, even though it may be fairly dull and effortful, leaves them feeling well enough almost to become an end in itself. Additionally, many women find a cosmetic value in the hopeful reduction of flab and even weight. All this has made exercise classes fairly popular, particularly since people find that the same exercises they would regard as intolerable when done alone can be performed in a group even with gusto.

QUESTION: Certainly not everybody is that way. I know men and women who haven't done a bit of exercise or sports in years. Is that bad for them?

ANSWER: We're all cut from slightly different cloth. Our needs are different—even those we're unaware of. I think there are people who enjoy good health, freedom from pain and fatigue even though they don't move much. If it works for them, I guess that's the answer. But I think most of us are often tired because of our *in*activity. It's not merely overwork which produces fatigue. Most of us enjoy a certain amount of activity and benefit from it. Often the activity bears no resemblance to exercise or sport. It may be dancing, a brisk walk, sculpting, painting a room, cleaning the attic. One of the most common exercises women indulge in is shopping and, during sales, it can become as physical and strenuous as a rugby match.

Many of our leisure-time activities give us a chance to use bodily equipment we don't have an opportunity to use routinely in our lives. We have certain sense organs, for example, having to do with balance which are only minimally used in sitting, standing, walking, lifting the phone and pushing a pencil. Skating, dancing, running, bicycling, skiing, all give us a chance to use these sense organs. But then, as I said a moment ago, we're not all the same. Survey a beach on a typical Sunday during the summer and you'll find people lying almost motionless soaking up the sun and others, in a state of perpetual motion, throwing a football, a frisbee, jumping in and out of the waves, playing volleyball, walking. Apparently they're all satisfying themselves.

QUESTION: Well, then, are you saying exercise is or isn't necessary?

ANSWER: I myself am on the side of motion, activity. It needn't be exercise per se but I believe that most of us benefit from the use of the body. There's an undeniable sense of exhilaration in motion. Some of us need more than we give ourselves; others overdo it. There is no one amount that's good for everybody. The thing to do is to listen more closely to the voice of your own body. I mean by that if you're always tired and take naps, obviously they're not working. Try some activity. If your activity doesn't do anything for you, try some rest. Once again, the magic clue is to look at the consequences of your behavior and then make a supreme effort to try new and different things.

QUESTION: Are we now ready for the sexy part of the chapter?

ANSWER: Well, the title reads "Eat—Drink—and Be Sexy." Obviously I displaced the word *merry.* I did this because I think sex is a most significant part of our physical life and I like to think of it as merry. Even though you don't recognize it, the fact is we've been talking about sex all along. People ordinarily don't think of eating, drinking, exercising or playing at sports as sexual activities, but they all have a great deal in common. If we look upon *sex as the use of the body for the purpose of pleasure,* it gets to be easy to see the connection. I even suspect there are more than mere elements of similarity in *all* our physical behavior. We may use our body more gratifyingly in one of these areas than others, but some of us seem to lend ourselves to physical expression more easily while others hold back. Physical activity, after all, is different from the uses of the mind. An occasional intellectual revelation may make us jump for joy, but generally the most complex profusion of ideas hardly shows up in overt acts of behavior. Like Rodin's *Thinker,* we sit through it all. We do this not so much without feeling as we do without manifest physical activity. Granted, eating, drinking and sexualizing don't involve the same gross physical behavior of exercise and athletics; there is, nonetheless, bodily activity and the feelings involved are dominated by an awareness of what our bodies are doing and the satisfaction or dissatisfaction it yields.

QUESTION: I never quite thought of it that way, but still I feel that sex is different, don't you?

ANSWER: Of course, it's different. Drinking is different from eating also. You don't chew the liquid you imbibe as you do your food. Exercising is different from athletics just as shadowboxing and sparring are different from throwing punches at your opponent in the ring. They're all different from each other in certain respects, but there are also similarities. All these activities are physical. This means, of course, that the body plays a large role in such activity. But the same is true of many kinds of good, honest work. The difference is in the consequences. Physical labor is undertaken to produce something material we want. Sex may be just as physical but it's just for pleasure. This bothered people, particularly during those long centuries before effective birth control. Lives were complicated, burdened, even ruined. It was easy to see pleasure as the work of the devil. Sex was denigrated as base and animal. But we don't have to choose between being human and animal. We're both. We have an animal side which provides us with opportunities for the pleasurable use of the body and we have a human side which offers us the opportunity to think, feel, modify our behavior and make judgments of it all. We needn't recoil with fear or loathing of our animal origins; we have the capacity to improve on them. We needn't any longer defile sex as some purely animal appetite. Nor need it be, as the Emperor Hadrian put it, "the mere rubbing of flesh together." This amounts to describing a violin sonata as the mere scraping of horsehair on catgut. Everything depends upon how the sonata is played. The same is true of sex, which ranges in expression from rape to acting out the most noble feelings of love.

But you're right in another respect. There are differences between the sexual use of the body and its other uses for pleasure. The others are much easier. It's easy, for example, to use one's body pleasurably by bicycling, jogging or skiing. You just go and do it. Sex is different in that it involves not just a piece of equipment but another person.

QUESTION: Immediately, I think of various sports you play with others. How's that different?

ANSWER: The difference is that the social-personal relationship in sports is minimal. Of course, you react to the personality of your opponent on the other side of the net and in some instances it may even dominate your game. Generally, I believe it's safe to say that your strokes and his strokes are far more important to the outcome than the interaction of your personalities. The extent to which a man and a woman involve themselves in sex also varies. We used to believe a man had to know a woman extremely well before she would permit him to go to bed with her. Today they have sex to get to know each other better. Love is no longer the condition for making love. Often having sex becomes a condition for love and for marriage itself. But before long, if not immediately, the activity, the sex, becomes subsumed under the general relationship. The interaction, in short, is not merely between two bodies but between two personalities. This makes sex very much more complicated than other sources of physical gratification, such as eating, exercising or playing at athletics. It's very much harder to develop and maintain the relationship between you and someone else than you and a tennis ball or you and a snow-packed slope. Sometimes it's the simpler activity that one wants. Over the long term, most agree, the complex, that is, the sexual relationship involves more of one's self. This is a way of saying that the physical and personal interaction we enjoy with someone else yields an even greater sense of fulfillment.

QUESTION: You needn't sell me on the idea of sex. I'm all for it. Much as I like sports I certainly feel there's more to sex. But so many people have problems with it. Can we talk about that a bit?

ANSWER: People have all kinds of problems. They get too easily upset by the hostility of others, they give in to gnawing fears, they feel they're not assertive enough, they all too often surrender to their shortcomings, they neglect some of their psychological needs, develop bad habits which make them miserable. And you're certainly right about sex. It seems to be a problem almost more often than a pleasure for people.

It's always the same. The problems get started innocently enough long before we see them as problems. For example, a mother feels it her duty to see that her baby eats what has been prescribed for him. In her persistence, she spoils what small part of eating he may enjoy. He becomes "a difficult child." She escalates her efforts with him. Conflict between them soon begins to characterize the tone of their relationship. It pervades other areas between them as the child grows. He may, with luck, come out of it all emotionally unscathed. He may also, through this first long-term relationship with a woman—his mother—learn *not* to get along well with women. This can easily have profound consequences for his sex life. The many links between the initial feeding problem and, ultimately, his sex life easily obscure the origins. But the origins are there—often in forms ostensibly unrelated to their subsequent appearance. Anyone can see the seeds in the apple; it's another matter to see the apple in the seeds. We're familiar with the origins of our grown-up behavior, all right, but when we see them as origins, we can't be sure of our predictions because of everything else that can and does happen—and during those beginnings we don't yet know what those events will be.

QUESTION: That makes it sound as though even informed parents can't avoid the pitfalls of early child care. Is it all that bad?

ANSWER: Not any more. I honestly believe that we've come to use our increased psychological understanding more each generation. There are far fewer uptight children today than we used to see clinically. There are fewer cases of forced feeding, fewer cases of children being punished for their early exploratory masturbation, fewer cases of children who grow up in a constricted, authoritarian world. Because of our permissiveness, we're making progress. But there's a lot more yet to be made. Every mistake that we make as parents does not leave an indelible impression upon the child. There are many good things we give our children, too. It's what comes out on *net balance* which counts and this is the extraordinarily complicated result of countless influences in the life of the growing child. After a while, his experiences *outside* the home begin to have a telling effect as well. But mostly I'm not interested here in what happened; explanation is only of secondary interest to me. It's what we can do about our sex life here and now that I regard as being of far greater importance. There's much in our early experiences we must learn to modify and outgrow in order to achieve true maturity. No matter how handicapped we may be by the traumas we suffer earlier in our lives, once we are old enough to take over, we've got to learn to do a better job for ourselves than was done for us. We needn't be what we are and we cannot afford to be what we were.

QUESTION: Well, what do you recommend?

ANSWER: Well, for starters I'd like to quote you. You said in effect just a little while ago that I didn't have to sell you on sex. You thought it was the best physical activity we had going. That attitude can do more for a healthy, fulfilling sex life than volumes of knowledge about it. In short, it's not what we know but how we feel because, in the final analysis, knowledge doesn't help us act nearly so easily as does feeling. And just as we act on our feelings, so also are our feelings influenced by our actions. The best way to alter our feelings about sex, or for that matter anything else, is not to trace out their origins and early development. That can take forever and leave us with little more than an understanding of how we got to feel the way we do. It's much easier *to do* things which can have the effect of improving our feelings no matter what their origins were.

QUESTION: I can't imagine what kind of things you want us to do. Certainly you can't recommend that we go out and be great lovers if we're not great lovers. I can still remember how difficult my first sexual contacts were during my teens. I died a thousand deaths.

ANSWER: But you did something about it—despite the fear, the trepidation, the agony you felt at the time. And if you hadn't done what you did, you wouldn't be nearly so far along with your sexual adjustment, isn't that so?

QUESTION: I guess you're right, but maybe I was lucky. Isn't it true that other people are traumatized by that first, or those first, experiences and they never get over it?

ANSWER: I think the role of trauma, that is, some strong, emotionally shocking experience, has been overplayed in our understanding of human nature. Our sense of the dramatic is often misleading. My own estimate is that those difficult early experiences with sex are virtually never the total explanation. But let me get on with my ideas about what can be done to improve a person's attitude toward sex, his feelings about it.

We've already made two points which should be helpful in this regard. First, that sex is not an individual activity. It involves another person, so that no matter how physical sex may be, there is also at least an element of personal interaction with someone else. Secondly, we pointed out that all kinds of early experiences which seem utterly irrelevant— even having been force-fed—can affect the relationship between a man and a woman, handicapping their sexual experience.

What this suggests is that there are many areas of our behavior which might need strengthening in order to improve our sex life. People make the mistake of going about it too narrowly. The same is true in sports. A tournament tennis player doesn't just practice his tennis strokes; he runs several miles a day and does all sorts of other exercises. He even finds ways to practice his concentration. If a person's attitude toward sex is handicapped by his feelings about his own body, there's a great deal he can do about it. If he feels hesitant and tongue-tied in the presence of women, he can practice becoming more fluent with women *in general* rather than just with those women he sees as sexual objects. A young woman who has been brought up in a strict home where sex was a dirty word can seek out less inhibited girlfriends and allow her association with them to help modify her attitudes.

Most important of all is to work on making oneself more interesting and acceptable to people. If you're fun to be with, people will be with you. And things happen, even if slowly, out of the relationship you develop. The trouble too often is that young men and women who are sexually starved because of their fears and self-doubt tend to come on too strong and scare each other off or do just the opposite, namely nothing. The thing to do initially is to work on the relationship. There's a good chance sex will follow in these permissive times. If a relationship is developed first, there is the additional advantage of minimizing the unadorned need to perform. Sex more easily becomes one among other things you do together for your mutual pleasure rather than for the purpose of proving oneself. It becomes part of a relationship rather than the whole of it. This alone makes it easier to maintain and offers more to enjoy.

QUESTION: You make it sound easy, but it really isn't, is it?

ANSWER: The directions are always easier than getting there. Like everything else, it's hardest to start but gets easier all the time. The reason this approach works is that it puts sex in perspective; it makes *sex part of a relationship*. It doesn't get out of proportion and loom before us as some terrifying obstacle. With this approach, we don't look at sex all by itself. No matter how sexy a man or a woman may be, you see that person *as a person* and not exclusively as a sex object. The interaction you develop is many-faceted. It feeds on your interests and strengths as a person, rather than depending exclusively on your sexual adequacy or inadequacy. As you develop a give-and-take with one another, sex gets to be a lot easier and more enjoyable.

QUESTION: That makes sense. If I understand you, you're saying that physical satisfaction is important to us, that we should use the bodies we have but that, as human beings, our social and psychological side has to be part of it. Would you say that's right?

ANSWER: I think that's very well put. It's true, the body is a great source of satisfaction and pleasure—*if* we use it properly. Eating can be the simplest natural pleasure we know. It can also be refined to the art of a gourmet. Unfortunately it can also be overdone more easily than other sources of physical fulfillment. Exercise and athletics give us the opportunity to use the body in a more strenuous, even violent, manner than is possible in the way we live and work as civilized human beings. Working up a sweat has a cathartic quality. This makes it psychologically as well as physically therapeutic. Additionally, athletic games allow us to act out fantasies, crowded out by the pressing reality of our jobs, but quietly feasible in play. This, too, is beneficial to our well-being.

Most of us will agree, I believe, that sex is one of the most driving and desirable of our appetites. Yet it's often the most fragile part of our life. Although eating and athletics ideally bring us into relationships with others, sex demands it. The fuller the relationship, the better the sex can be because, in addition to the purely physical joy it provides, it also becomes one of the most meaningful expressions of love. But many people have limited capacity for love. They find others troublesome. They can enjoy sex immensely, but not with the same person for long. For a while, they believe they chose poorly. Some eventually get to see they love poorly. Generally, the quality of a sexual relationship reflects the kind of personal interaction that exists between a man and a woman. It deteriorates or improves accordingly. Sex cannot be learned like a recipe or practiced like a golf swing. Orgasm is not guaranteed merely by greater know-how and effort. People need to be free of unhealthy attitudes about their own bodies and about sex. Most of all, the personal obstacles that prevent us from accepting and being accepted by others must be minimized. Anyone who wants to enjoy sex for the long term must learn not only to like sex, but to like people. But it's not an all-or-none matter. Some enjoy it more, some less and most of us enjoy it more sometimes than others. We don't get better at it by working narrowly and specifically on the how-to of sex. We get better with people in general and members of the opposite sex in particular. And it all starts by increasing our satisfaction with ourselves through the efforts we make toward becoming ever more interesting to others.

QUESTION: You said something a while back which I want to bring up, namely that we can't trade our body in for a new model the way we do our automobiles. That emphasizes the need for care and maintenance. But I have the feeling you mean something more. Am I right?

ANSWER: Yes, you are. Of course it's important to maintain the functional ability of our body. We *feel* good physically when we move effortlessly. Additionally, we *look* good and, in our social world, the bonus is approval. Finally, there is an underlying sense of self-approval and acceptance in being what one wants to be: healthy, good-looking and able—not carried to the extreme as an end in itself but as part of our effort to make ourselves, our relationships and life attractive. This is how we improve our image of ourself, our interest in others and our very enjoyment of life.

CHAPTER
11

Marriages Get Better or Worse—or Better *and* Worse—But They Never Stay the Same

QUESTION: I must say that's a rather odd title. I'm sure everyone agrees with the first part of it; the second is somewhat confusing, that a marriage can get *both* better and worse at the same time; and the third . . . well, I never quite thought of it that way, but I suspect you're right: a marriage doesn't remain the same. This would mean, then, that a good marriage is one that is frequently being remade—by the same people. Right?

ANSWER: Right! A long time ago there was a Greek philosopher, Heraclitus by name, who believed that *everything* is subject to change. Only it's not all in one direction. Some things wear down with use, others improve with age. And when it comes to human relationships, both can happen at the same time. People don't just live happily ever after when they get married, nor do they find that the blush is off the bloom once the honeymoon is over. Of course, it goes without saying that some relationships remain more the same than others. A highly structured work relationship, for example, between an employer and an employee, is bound to be very different from the relationship of friends, lovers or members of the same family. In the one case, a very small part of one's personality is involved and in the other, the whole range of our feelings and emotions is allowed expression. As a result there are bound to be many more ups and downs in the more intimate relationship.

QUESTION: You're right. I see it at once. The closer we are to anyone, the better we're going to get along. And, also, the worse we're going to get along. In that sense, it doesn't stay the same. Is that what you mean?

ANSWER: That's part of it. I think we'll all agree that the closer a relationship, the more fulfilling—but, also, it's not without episodes of disappointment and heartache. There are times a man sees his wife as the very embodiment of understanding, compassion, tenderness and love and yet, at other times, even during the same day, he may wonder how she could be so thoughtless, self-centered and detached. Similarly, women often find their husbands warm, giving and generous and, at other times, agonize over being neglected and hurt by the same man. Even in a single day, the marital relationship seems to change before our very eyes. But when I say it never stays the same, I also mean that as we grow, or at least, age, we change somewhat—sometimes even drastically —and it's inevitable that the marital relationship changes with us. A man succeeds or fails in his business, changes his job, goes into politics, has an extramarital affair—any of these things can change his orientation toward his relationship with his wife. Nowadays the same thing happens to a woman and her attitude toward her husband changes also. And even without major changes in the lives of husband and wife, some relationships start with better stock or are nurtured differently from others.

QUESTION: Better stock? What do you mean by that?

ANSWER: Well, it's like buying plants at a nursery. Some are simply better than others, even though they sell for the same price. Similarly, any number of human beings can be equally attractive premaritally as the plants looked originally. But the more emotionally stable, that is, the better adjusted, like plants of better stock, can survive the changes we're talking about a lot better. I've often felt that a marriage is as stable or as well-adjusted as the people in it. This is not to say that those people who don't enjoy the benefits of great emotional stability are second-rate in any way; not at all. A man can be a titan of industry, a great artist or musician or, even more simply, just a nice guy and still have little patience or ability to cope with some of the emotional disappointments of a close relationship with another human being. Additionally, there are many people who come out of homes where the prevailing pattern of life was that of emotional conflict and upset. The language of their behavior could not help but develop that accent. They never really learned how to nurture a relationship. And, given today's freedoms, their emphasis is on what they feel they *don't* have to put up with rather than on the patience and restraint necessary for resolving difficulties.

QUESTION: You make it sound as though problems in marriage are inevitable. Is that what you really believe?

ANSWER: That's a fairly glum assessment, even if true. Let's put it this way. If we agree that change is the rule in marriage, that marriages *do* get better or worse, or better and worse, and that they never stay the same, then it has to follow that for a marriage to succeed there must be no end of constant readjustments. Isn't that so? We don't solve a couple of problems and live happily ever after, any more than we get married and live happily ever after. Such romantic nonsense is utterly misleading and totally unrealistic. Nobody is just blissfully happy all of the time—either alone or with somebody else. People of emotional maturity and stability have problems, just as good marriages have problems. I've pointed out again and again that such people have more problems in fact than the neurotic. The latter is stuck with the *same* problem for so long that he loses his sense of freedom. He suffers overly much for anything he achieves because of the weight of his problem.

QUESTION: Now you make it sound as though it's perfectly normal to have problems.

ANSWER: Of course it is. Just as it is normal to feel fourteen pounds of pressure against every square inch of our bodies. We've been led down the primrose path to believe that if we achieve enough emotional maturity and stability, the rest of our lives will be spent in paradise. Nothing could be further from the truth. The good life not only involves solving problems, but solving them again and again and again. *It's the ability to solve our problems that is the hallmark of good adjustment.* To dream of a condition in which all your problems are solved is, well, to dream. That's all. Granted we're brought up in a society where the very word *problem* has an unhealthy, unsavory sound. But that too is misleading. The problem itself doesn't stand for unhappiness. Only an unresolved problem does. With the ability to cope, problems don't remain long enough to get under our skin.

QUESTION: I'm beginning to see that yours is a much more realistic approach. Could you possibly make it even more concrete by giving me an example?

ANSWER: Fine. Let's take the case of a couple who have been married for approximately fifteen years, and trace the history of their sexual adjustment (and readjustment) over that period of time to illustrate what I mean. Tom and Dorothy dated for a little over a year before they got married, during which time the sexual attention they paid each other increased until they actually began to sleep together after the first month or two. They both described their sexual relationship as thrilling, exciting, fantastic during that period of time. For the first year or two of marriage they believed their relationship remained very much the same except that they sensed the beginnings of a routine quality to it. Although this took the edge somewhat off their sex life together, they still had no strong complaints about it.

Much of the third year of their marriage, Dorothy was pregnant. They were both more than a little concerned about harming the fetus in intercourse so that there was more abstinence than indulgence of whatever remained of their sexual appetites at the time. Although they made some effort to recoup their sex life after the birth of their first child, Dorothy was giving so much of herself to the chores of motherhood that she was generally tired and not very interested in sex. The following year she was pregnant again. And the next two years seemed also to be usurped by the demands of her two babies. It's not that their sex life was totally lost during this period of time. They continued to get along well enough together out of bed to enjoy being in bed together. It's just that whereas earlier in their sex life together they couldn't seem to get enough of each other, now sex was brief, intermittent and all-too-familiar.

It was, in fact, when they had been married seven years that Tom had begun to feel the itch characteristic of the period. He began to notice how many pretty girls there were around. Many of his business associates spoke so enthusiastically about their sexual conquests as to make it all sound very inviting. It's true, he'd sort of gotten used to Dorothy. He liked her and she was even prettier than most, but he had gotten used to her. The temptations were becoming very real to him, but Tom knew he wanted a good marriage. He liked the life that went with it. He could remember his life as a bachelor. It was fine for a while; then he tired of it. It wasn't out of some moral predisposition that he decided to work on the sex life of his marriage; it was just that he realized he wanted more than he had.

And so he began to court his wife again, in a sense. The first time he brought flowers home, Dorothy even kidded him by asking what he was guilty about. His reply, though equally joking, had enough truth in it to be effective. He said, "I felt evil thoughts coming on and that was enough." It was enough for Dorothy to respond to his sexual urging later that evening. Still later, lying in each other's arms together, they realized there ought to be more of what they had just enjoyed together. Of course, the children, his job, their house, their social life, all continued to make excessive demands on them and their sex life began to slip away again. Tom hit upon the effective idea of treating his wife like a date. He would have her meet him for drinks—as he might have if it were someone else. They'd arrange for baby sitters and have dinners out more often together. They worked on establishing a certain amount of freedom from the children, which not only made them better parents when they actually were with them, but gave them time to enjoy each other more.

During this period of time, there was also a decline in censorship in society and a general loosening up of sexual morality. Dorothy, who used to think of many aspects of lovemaking as too difficult for her to handle—even though she did not quite regard them perverse—now began to take a different attitude toward them. Tom was delighted to find her willing to experiment with oral sex. One thing led to another and before long, the last vestiges of Dorothy's sexual inhibitions were finally dissolved. The orgasm that she had been feigning for years was now real and, with that, she became a more avid sexual partner than ever. Today after fifteen years of marriage their sex life is far better than it was during that premarital period which they described as thrilling, exciting, fantastic.

QUESTION: I think I see what you mean. Originally part of their adjustment to each other, namely their sex life, was good; then it dwindled; then they worked on it, made it pretty fair again, worked on it some more and wound up making it even better than it was originally. This is what you mean, I gather, by continuous readjustments. Is that so?

ANSWER: Exactly so.

QUESTION: But are you implying that if he had had an extramarital affair, it would necessarily have been damaging to the marriage?

ANSWER: Not necessarily, but more frequently than not, it does have a damaging effect. One reason is that men tend to make—or to allow—the extramarital affair to become more than merely sexual. This tends to complicate their lives, increasing their problems rather than resolving them. A man who can't get along with one woman doesn't find it any easier to get along with two. The other impelling reason that makes the affair inimical to marriage is that it reinforces the man's impulses toward freedom, that is, his tendency *not* to improve what he has, but to keep seeking satisfaction elsewhere. His marriage, once the object of his dreams and desires, becomes an obstacle rather than a source of satisfaction. The sense of obligation and guilt that remain are enough to defeat the likelihood of much pleasure, sexual or not, at home. Very often, the extramarital relationship itself is soured by this very development in a man's feelings. He's chosen a solution which, in failing to work for *him,* fails to work for his marriage—or his affair.

QUESTION: I'm sure there are lots of couples who want to work at the difficulties their relationship presents but don't know how. Isn't that so?

ANSWER: Unfortunately, that is very much so. In no other human relationship do people talk so much and do so little, to their detriment, as in marriage. In virtually every troubled marriage, the woman complains that her husband never talks to her and the man complains that his wife is constantly making things worse by bringing up their painful problem again and again. The fact of the matter is that they're both correct. It's not much of a relationship when people have little to share verbally with each other and it's an equally poor relationship when they argue over the same problem again and again with little or no change.

QUESTION: But I thought it was good to get things out rather than to allow them to fester inside of us. I'd be surprised to hear you disagree with that.

ANSWER: Of course, I can't help but agree that when something unexpressed festers within us, it will not get better by itself and, in fact, frequently worsens with time. However, I am not at all sure that merely expressing what bothers us has any great therapeutic effect. It's kind of stylish these days to believe that letting it all hang out is good for our mental health. But style never monopolized truth, wisdom or pragmatic efficiency. Over three-quarters of a century ago, Sigmund Freud discovered that people with emotional difficulties frequently had things bottled up inside of them. But not even he recommended just getting it all out—that is, except in a psychoanalyst's office. Even then, he made it very clear that only very elaborate and sophisticated sublimations would work. What he meant by that was that we had to find personally and socially acceptable means of expressing what bothered us, rather than merely blurting it all out.

QUESTION: Now that you mention it, I do see how merely telling someone what bothers you about him doesn't really change much, does it?

ANSWER: Getting it out of your system or giving it to him straight from the shoulder rarely has the cathartic effect you hoped it would. What generally happens is that the other person gets his hackles up. And why shouldn't he? In effect, you're being critical of him and inviting him to defend himself. And more frequently than not, that's exactly what he does—with equal emotional fervor, which soon escalates into the kind of confrontation that settles nothing. The mere public spillage of feeling doesn't really get rid of that feeling, even if you enjoy a certain vindictive satisfaction at the moment. The chances are you'll tell the story again and again to others and remain just as dissatisfied with the behavior of the person you confronted. In short, the worst thing you can do with someone who bothers you is to sit down and tell him about all the ways in which he is amiss and how he bothers you. Yet, all too often this is exactly what husbands and wives who have problems together do.

QUESTION: I understand what you're saying and I realize that it's not effective to have such verbal confrontations, but how else can one go about it?

ANSWER: I'd like to underscore the fact that these confrontations don't work. Let's return to the couple we spoke of a little while ago and examine what might have happened if Dorothy and Tom had faced each other in this fashion. Suppose Tom very bravely faced up to the issue when their sex life had begun to dwindle and he up and told Dorothy how he felt. To be utterly realistic about it, chances are he would not have chosen a perfectly pleasant evening they shared together and then presented the issue to her with concern and compassion. That isn't how it happens. He gets annoyed over something else that she does—something fairly trivial—and begins to grouse about it; one thing leads to another and then, when he finally brings up the sexual matter, he doesn't merely tell her about it, he *complains* about it. In fact, the chances are he does even worse than that, he *accuses* her of lack of sexual interest. But whether he does it well or poorly, at least he gets it out into the open. If she's offended enough by his accusation, there's a very good chance that she in turn will accuse him of unimaginative, routine lovemaking. She might even add some expressions of bitterness over the lack of understanding she feels he shows in his failure to appreciate how much she has to do with the baby these days. There's a good chance that what follows develops increasing heat, but no sexual ardor.

But let's say Tom did, in fact, present the matter in a more loving fashion and Dorothy, in turn, responded equally tenderly and agreed that they do something about it. The sober fact of the matter is that *only what they do about it, rather than what they said or even agreed to,* is going to make a difference. And doing something about it would actually be more effective *without* the preliminary discussion. The reason is that once they've talked about it, either Dorothy or Tom could easily be left with the unanswered haunting question: Is she acting this way because she really feels it or is it a command performance? Is he really satisfied now or does he still feel there's something wrong? Even verbal reassurances might not be totally effective in removing these doubts.

QUESTION: But isn't it true that having brought up and discussed the matter was the first step in getting them to act on their problem and that, without that, they might never have acted on it?

ANSWER: Once again I'm afraid I agree and disagree with the implications of your question. Yes, it is true that, *in this instance,* talking about it promoted some activity which helped. But it doesn't always happen this way. I sorely suspect that, more often than not, all that discussion breeds is repeated discussion and, as they blame each other more, their alienation increases. This is true for any problem and sex is particularly difficult because people are so touchy about it. Even though a person feels very modern and sophisticated in being able to talk about sex, the truth of the matter is that most people feel more than a little uncomfortable with such discussion. Taking the sexual problem in hand really does not require the kind of preliminary discussion which, in this case, helped somewhat.

People ideally have an influence upon each other—otherwise there's little or no relationship. We exercise this influence not by fiat—not by telling people what we want from them. We don't merely say, "Let there be light" as the Lord did in the beginning. Of course it's easier that way, but you've got to be the Lord to do it. Limited to our human devices, we subtly manipulate the circumstances around us. We even manipulate—in the good sense of the word—the people. For example, Tom sees that his wife is worn out at the end of each day and so he insists on getting some help for her. Additionally, he helps with the dinner, they eat at a later hour under more romantic circumstances. Perhaps they share a bottle of wine. He directs the conversation skillfully, just as he would if he were trying to make out with a date; it arouses his wife's romantic interests once again.

QUESTION: I've got to interrupt at this point. Do you really believe all this is necessary in a marriage?

ANSWER: Most certainly I do. There's no magic in the words, "I do." They don't guarantee the quality of a wife's sexual behavior for the rest of her married life. The fact is, they guarantee nothing. Remember I said earlier that life is a series of constant readjustments. We've got *to make* what we want, not just demand or expect it. We don't just "luck" into things. Life isn't a series of discoveries so much as inventions and creations. And why should we be so surprised by the need for charm in our own household? Don't we, after all, enjoy being charming? Certainly it's not too much of an effort. It shouldn't be if we're what we want to be.

QUESTION: Okay, okay. It's just that I never thought of it that way. But I still say it sounds like a lot of effort.

ANSWER: Living is a lot of effort. We feel it less when we make it habitual. That's really the trick in creating the good life, namely *to learn to do all of the things that work well for us so habitually that the feeling of effort approaches nil.* It's the opposite of being neurotic, where the cost of living in terms of effort and emotional upset is always high. To put it even more simply, we don't get what we want by crying for it, demanding it or merely talking about it. Notice I said *merely* talking about it. The only way we can hope to be successful when we tell people what we don't like about them or what we want from them is for us to talk in the most extraordinarily persuasive, uncontentious, convincing way possible. Needless to say, very few of us are such good talkers. Our tendency is to find fault and *blame* someone for our dissatisfaction, rather than launching ourselves on a difficult, seductive sales campaign.

It may be hard to believe, but it's easier to *do something differently yourself* with a person than to talk persuasively with him. A woman can make her husband's favorite dessert, even though she's angry with him, very much more easily than she can talk gently about a sensitive area with him precisely because she's angry with him. A man can bring his wife a present even though he's furious with her for something she did the previous day, but he cannot nearly so easily sit down and talk about that issue without failing to show his anger. This is really the most dependable and effective way of altering each other's feelings—by *doing* something different which is aimed at pleasing the person. Once we are assured of rapport all over again, discussion *may* become tolerable. I still put it that tentatively because it's always easy to back into a hornets' nest when we discuss what we'd like to have from each other.

QUESTION: But you also said earlier that men and women in marriage also make the mistake of not talking enough to each other. What did you mean by that?

ANSWER: Well, I should think there's more to talk about than what displeases us about each other in marriage. Ideally a marriage grows, as does any relationship, by the opportunities people enjoy to share something. Marriage, being a far more intimate relationship than any other, offers the opportunity for more of this sharing. After all, much of the life of a husband and wife is also spent apart from each other and, unless they tell each other what they've done during those periods of time, their relationship together at home remains fairly thin. If a man comes home day after day and does little more than have dinner, bury his head in the newspaper, glue himself to the TV and then go to bed, he soon becomes little more than a stranger to his own wife.

In addition to their occupation, people of resources have

manifold interests and generally love to talk about these activities. And they share many of them as well. Even the
almost inescapable attention we give the world, as it is
brought to us through the various media, is something that
people of vitality talk about. If the only time a husband and
wife sit down and talk is when they have a problem with
themselves or their children or their jobs, their relationship
seems limited to all the *unpleasant* things in life.

*People grow together by talking to each other—but not about
each other.* It's different at first because when they met initially there was a great deal of exploration of each other. But
having done that, unless they continue to share their thoughts
and feelings with each other about anything and everything,
all they'll know is about each other's past. As a matter of fact,
one might even use as an index of the quality of a marriage
the ease or difficulty with which the couple continue to
speak to each other. Once they run out of things to say to
each other, their marriage is virtually dead.

QUESTION: I can see how talking about problems is a drag
and I also see now, given your reasons for it, that merely
talking about them doesn't get rid of them. Frankly, I still
don't see how people can avoid it. I can't blame a disgruntled
husband or wife for bringing up the issues that bother them
in the marriage. It's almost as unrealistic as expecting a woman who has just discovered her husband is fooling around not
to say anything to him about it. Am I being unreasonable?

ANSWER: Absolutely not—even though I am not so sure, in
the example you've just cited, that the best thing a woman
could do on the discovery of her husband's infidelity is to
confront him with it. I grant you there are countless trying
moments in life when it's almost too much to expect people to
control themselves and do what's best for them. I have no
difficulty understanding why a person should explode or even
in justifying it in terms of how unfairly he has been set upon.
Of course, a woman is deeply hurt on learning of her
husband's extramarital escapades and morality is totally on

her side. But as a psychologist, I'm neither a friend who clucks sympathetically over someone's anguish nor am I a judge dispensing fairness and justice. *I'm interested in determining what works best for people.*

A person can be in the right, justified in his moral disapproval of someone, and yet be acting against his own best interests. The woman who upbraids her husband in moral indignation may be very effective as a judge—she does succeed in adding to his guilt—but at the same time she makes herself less attractive as a wife or, at least, as a woman. She's not meeting the competition; she's encouraging it. Additionally, she's merely reacting to the end result of a whole series of causes which she's failing to consider. The only effective treatment of her husband's life *outside his marriage* has to do with things between them *in the marriage.*

QUESTION: Of course, you're right. But still aren't you expecting too much of us? Certainly you don't see people as all that rational and mature, do you?

ANSWER: No, of course not. If they were, I'd be out of business. Although we have the potential for great rationality in our thought and even in our behavior, it's the animal side of us that keeps me in business. People need a lot of help to act out their rational potential. Part of that help is what I'm trying to get you to accept here in this book. I've been trying to help you develop the habit of seeing the consequences of *your own* behavior. Mostly we're interested in being right, justified. It sounds very noble, but it's not very effective. There are other ways of looking at things. We've been schooled in the necessity of being right and justified and I grant you it's often very important. It's in our personal life, in any close relationship, that being right and justified doesn't always leave us feeling better. Sure, it's always someone else's fault but if we know people are sometimes disappointing, shouldn't we learn how *not* to add to the hurt?

Things have a way of happening—often when we least expect them. The animal side of us gives rise to passions that are

difficult to control. Often the best we do with this situation is
to declare our innocence and prove we're right. All this may
well be so, but it also denounces the other party as wrong,
guilty, thoughtless, hurtful, and so on. In short, being hurt,
we lash out and become hurtful. It's understandable that we
should act this way, but is it good for us? Does it help alter
the conditions that brought the painful situation about?

   Your point is well taken. I don't expect mere men and
women to act like gods. I know that even mature people have
many immature moments, but I am saying the more we look
at *not* the rightness and justification of our behavior but rather *its consequences for us,* the more habitual it becomes and
the more we will act in *our best interests.* After a while the
strain and effort that self-control usually exerts on us gets to
be replaced by the automaticity of habit. It begins to feel easy
and natural to do what's best for us.

QUESTION: I like that and I can even see myself working on
it. In a sense, you're sort of redefining maturity for me in
down-to-earth terms. If I learn to see the consequences of my
behavior habitually, then instead of just doing things impulsively, I'll be able to pick and choose those actions which
are best for me. I like that. Is there any other concrete suggestion you might make in helping me achieve this?

ANSWER: For quite a long while, until the habit begins to
set within you, I strongly recommend that when untoward
things happen, *do or say nothing momentarily.* This, of course,
won't stop you from *feeling* upset; just don't do anything
about it—if possible. With the sudden flare-up of feeling and
emotion, you can't be expected to see the consequences of
what you might do—not initially. And so it's best to wait
until the smoke clears before you're able to pick and choose
the behavior that is in your best interest. It's like a definition
of public relations I once came upon that suggests you write
the angry letter tomorrow—for obvious reasons.

QUESTION: I guess what you're saying is that what's true for public relations is also true for private relations. I still have difficulty accepting the idea that we have to be as guarded, as aware, as careful, as hardworking at home, in marriage, as we have to be in our outside relationships.

ANSWER: Suppose you decide to have a house built for yourselves. What do you do? Do you just come upon a design, a type of house, and fall in love with it and tell your architect or contractor, "That's it. Build it"? The fact is, you begin to make changes even on the drawing board. And this continues during the construction process, after you've moved in and forever after that. The same is pretty much true of marriage. Our tastes, dreams and expectations keep changing more than we're aware of. Of course, it's disappointing to find that the person you married is not the one you thought you did. But *we're* not the same from one period of our lives to another.

It may be true, as the French say, that "the more things change, the more they remain the same." But to be happy, we can't settle for that. We've got to find ways of satisfying our transient and superficial needs as well. We do this not merely by resolving to or expecting to live happily ever after following marriage. We do it by looking at our marriage as part of a life which itself is constantly changing. We needn't be, as you put it, guarded, careful and all that hardworking about it, but we do have to work at it. Yesterday's solutions don't always fit today's problems. The more clearly we see this, the more fully does life become a process that's never finished. And it's good that way. Otherwise there's nothing left to do but sit and ruminate over the past.

I would like to leave you with two highly important suggestions—virtual mandates—of how to go about this process in marriage:

1. No matter how searingly painful the problem may be that arises between husband and wife, it is essential you do everything you can to *maintain favorable attitudes toward each other.* Treat yourselves and each other well no matter how unfavorably disposed you

may be to each other at any moment! I know this is hard, but there are many critical moments in life when it is absolutely essential that we divorce our behavior from our feelings. This is how we write the angry letter—tomorrow. Our problems don't always demand immediate attention. We handle them a lot better by going out and cooling off a little first.

2. A mandate of equal importance is to learn once and for all that even the best-intended discussions of your problem will more than likely degenerate into hurtful encounters. If you insist on saying something, *learn how to say you're sorry.* I recommend this even if you don't feel it—because it may help restore some willingness to do something constructive about the problem. And the fact is, there is something to express sorrow about, whether you feel right or wrong, in the hurt feelings present. It's the idlest kind of wishful thinking to believe you'd be happy if only your mate understood you or didn't do those things that upset you.

It's much more realistic to believe that your wife is someone whom you found attractive and loved, but who does these dopey things. How can you modify yourself or her so that things will run more smoothly between you? The more oriented to *doing* things we become, the more at one we also become with reality itself. It's in this way that we eventually entertain the pleasant prospect of enjoying ourselves more together all of the time, instead of dully getting used to each other or constantly discovering more and more that's wrong. The best marriage is not the one you *made,* but the one you *constantly make and remake.*

QUESTION: But isn't it true that the better the husband and wife understand each other, the better they can get along?

ANSWER: Not at all. People can come to understand each other and not at all like what they see. They may regard the differences as irreconcilable. Sure, a man *potentially* benefits from knowing how his wife typically reacts and feels about many things—particularly things in him. But this remains a mere possibility unless, in addition to what he knows about her, he also has the willingness and ability to act on it. In many instances, this means giving up many of his own long-standing habits and cherished attitudes and values. If he's not inclined to do this, his understanding of his wife eventually forms the bill of particulars for his divorce. We seem to be going through a period now in psychological history which involves us in a veritable compulsion to know, to understand. I wouldn't be so averse to this if it didn't crowd out the equally, if not more important, elements of willingness and ability to act. People all too often, as a result, castigate rather than caress each other with their understanding. They tell each other what's wrong with less and less compassion, and the more disappointed they feel in each other, the less willing and able they are to do anything about it—short of worsening their relationship. When you get right down to it, people can't be counted on to get along *all* the time or even to understand each other *all* the time. The strength of their relationship ultimately depends on what they *do* about it at these times.

QUESTION: Are you saying that the best thing a man can do when his wife is upset is merely to give in? To say she's right and apologize?

ANSWER: It certainly is helpful for starters to tell a woman how sorry you are for having upset her. There may even be times—many times—when it's expeditious to say she's right and you're wrong even if you don't deeply feel it! Even more effective would be to employ some diversionary tactic to avoid the issue of who's right and who's wrong. Let's illustrate what I mean. A man comes in at midnight when he said he'd be home at nine or nine-thirty. He's obviously had some drinks and his wife has imagined the worst. He had told her he was going to be out with some clients but when he returns home three hours later than he said he would and is feeling no pain, she's furious. This is a poor time for him to discuss the merits of entertaining clients, the essential innocence of it or for that matter anything of what happened that evening. The chances of winning when you plead your case against a prejudiced jury are very small indeed. Assuming the man is innocent—although, even if he weren't, it would still be the best thing to do—a little white lie might serve as the diversionary tactic I referred to. "I'm sorry I didn't phone again from the restaurant to tell you I'd be delayed, but it was just too difficult. But believe me, I kept pressing to get these men back to their hotel. What I wanted to tell you was what a really nice place I found it to be and that I made a reservation for tomorrow night for the two of us. I was thinking how much you'd enjoy it and already I was visualizing the good time we'd have tomorrow. Come on, now, dry your eyes, let's have a cup of tea and tell me about your day."

QUESTION: There's something about that I just don't like. I don't know if it's the deception or the lack of manliness in not standing up for what he knows is right.

ANSWER: I'm not surprised by your reaction because I've heard it countless times before. It goes without saying we all have our prejudices. principles or moral hang-ups, some of which are necessary buttresses for our self-image. Often these attitudes prompt us to evaluate an event in such a way that we are more interested in *standing up for ourselves* than in determining *where it takes us*.

Suppose the husband in this case is truly innocent and feels, as a matter of principle, that if he doesn't stand up to his wife then and there, he's being something less than a man. This is what I mean by acting out one's ideas of *what one should be* versus taking a course of action that leads you *where you want to be*. The chances are the argument which follows would last well into the night—if not into the morning. Both husband and wife would be left drained and I doubt very much that there would be a clear-cut winner. Both acted

out what they felt necessary for *themselves—not the relationship.* I also doubt that either one felt rewarded by the
choice they made of handling the situation that way.

I like to think that what comes out in the end, what's on the
bottom line, is important. The way I see it, the woman's attack initially was reckless. If she was really concerned about
losing his affection, it would be foolish to berate him and
expect him to be all-loving for it. By attacking him for his still
unproven infidelity, she not only makes herself less attractive
to him but even puts the idea in his head, if he hasn't already
thought of it. And if it is true that he is running around, she's
not going to win him over this way either. Of course, the
situation is threatening for her. It not only involves the deep
hurt of rejection, of having been lied to, but possibly the
future of her economic security as well. When someone is
upset enough, it's easy to explode in a fashion that is utterly
unhelpful. All the more reason to do nothing initially and
wait until you regroup your thoughts and feelings on the subject. The fact of the matter is that marriage today is no longer
the rigid, confining structure it once was. It's now more im-
pressionable, more vulnerable to outside forces, even competitive ones, than ever before.

QUESTION: Are you suggesting that whenever anything disturbing happens in a marriage that the thing to do should be
more for the relationship than for the individuals in it?

ANSWER: Yes, that's a good, concise way of putting it. It
should be *initially* more for the relationship than for the individuals. This is quite a reversal of our current emphasis on
letting it all hang out, on doing what we feel, on doing our
own thing and letting the chips fall where they may. Of
course, anything we do for the relationship has to be done
through the people in it in order to make the relationship
work for us. The simplest and most effective thing to do is to
maintain a *willingness* in the people for the relationship; that
is, a desire for it. The reason this is so essential is that any
relationship can easily and quickly degenerate into little more

than opportunity for blaming our unhappiness on someone. It's fairly obvious that the most effective way of maintaining the relationship initially is by assuaging the feelings of the hurt party. Ideally this should take precedence over the blustering expression of one's own feelings. I say this for the simple reason that if our own feelings remain our *primary* concern—and, for many people, their *exclusive* concern—the relationship is a very weak one, if it exists at all. Initially we expect our hurt feelings to be soothed by love, but it's important to develop a more reliable variety of this kind of balm out of self-restraint and habit. Unfortunately, we can't always expect a lover to be loving when he's hurt or upset. Habit is more dependable.

QUESTION: A while back, when you introduced the subject of extramarital relations for merely illustrative purposes, I thought of something I wanted to ask; perhaps now is the time. Is an extramarital affair always damaging to a marriage or, on the contrary, might it conceivably help people over certain rough spots and preserve a marriage?

ANSWER: It goes without saying that it's extremely difficult to get bona fide statistics on the frequency and effects of extramarital relations. The built-in need for secrecy is enough to vitiate the validity of most any survey. On the other hand, we "know" that it has become more common than ever. But we also know that not all people who stray from their marriage necessarily get a divorce. It follows, then, that not all cases of marital infidelity break up a marriage. Whether or not they even damage a marital relationship depends on the individuals and the conduct of their affair. I think it's safe to say that if it is discovered, there is unavoidable hurt for the party betrayed. Some people get over it and wind up caring more than ever for their marital partner. Others never do and, in some instances, may even maintain a vendetta which can become more ruinous to the marriage secondarily than the affair itself was in the first place. But even this doesn't necessarily lead to separation and divorce. There are people we know who will cut off their own noses to prevent the happiness of someone else.

As for the conduct of the affair itself, the most general way in which that becomes damaging to the marriage is by the failure to keep it compartmentalized. So long as it remains a *part* of one's life, a sort of extra, added attraction, one can maintain the discretion necessary for a secret alliance. But as soon as our feelings get out of hand and we want more, the affair grows and becomes so demanding as to interfere with the rest of our life. That's when we get into trouble. In other words, when the extra, added attraction becomes the main feature, the distribution of our time and effort undergoes a change, too. Longing and desperateness take the place of acceptance of less and a willingness to keep things in order. Once anyone allows the affair to get out of hand this way, it easily becomes an addiction, a compulsion, which no longer offers the escape it did earlier from one's humdrum marital existence. While the affair was an *additive,* life was momentarily brightened by it. As a *replacement,* it can make life more miserable than ever.

QUESTION: As I understand you, you're saying that although an affair need *not* be injurious to marriage, it very often is. Correct?

ANSWER: Yes, sir—and for still another reason. I suspect that once a person has an affair, he or she is prone to have another one. The reason is that with each affair, there is something of a loss in our motivation to work out our happiness any more fully within the givens of married life. There's a tendency instead to turn elsewhere. Once we do this, we also become increasingly perceptive of the opportunities elsewhere. Typically a young woman may live with her marriage for some years before she even develops an awareness of the attentions other men have been giving her. Often too, her inexperience prompts her initially to recoil in moral judgment —of the men and herself. I feel that the inevitability of it all is constantly on the increase in today's world. Our education, our affluence and the changes in our values have sharpened and increased our expectations. We want a great deal more out of life than in other historic periods we thought possible.

But there is an emptiness and a weariness that remains in it for many just the same. So what does a man do about his unfulfilled life? He can't risk quitting his job. Nor does he simply walk out on his wife and children. Taking up a new occupation isn't feasible. Go back to school? It's too late. Get a sailboat, a sports car, a new set of golf clubs? After a moment of exhilaration, life stays pretty much the same even with these things. Another woman? One who responds to his dreams. That's it! The one he has, his wife, responds to the *facts* of his life: his emptiness, failure, dissatisfaction as well as his dreams which have a more remote quality. A new woman is initially taken with what he wants even more than with what he has. She sees promise, excitement, even beauty in it and him. Ergo, the easiest escape from one's own emotional failures is an extramarital affair! And today, given the permissiveness with which man-woman relationships develop, this happens with more and more men and women all the time. Some find brief satisfaction in a new taste thrill. Some even find a new life. Most find complication and eventual disappointment. The glumness of this opinion must not be mistaken for moral disapproval. My own attitude is to live and let live. This leaves room in one's ultimate judgment only for what works, that is, for what works best for each and every individual. What a person does is not so important in the final analysis as what *it* (the double life) does—*for* him and *to* him. How he conducts himself generally determines whether or not it will eventuate in his best interests.

QUESTION: I begin to realize more clearly than before how much we and our marriages change over the years. It's not just age itself; so much happens—children, changes in business, location, friends, the ups and downs we have with each other. I guess that's why there are so many divorces, wouldn't you say?

ANSWER: Frankly, I think there are lots of divorces because they're finally easy to get today. The absence of divorces years ago did not signal good marriages. All it registered was that divorce was too hard, except for a few, to get. Today we're also closer to ourselves and what we want. But even that's more verbal than expressed unconditionally in our behavior. Look around at the married couples you know at a dinner party and ponder the question: Would they marry each other today if they weren't married? The chances are that even fewer than we think would. Yet by and large, they don't get a divorce even if they wouldn't remarry.

Despite the high divorce rate, many people continue to live with and work at their marriage. In many, an inner voice prompts them to wonder how much better it would be with someone else. It's easy to fantasize on the initial delights of some change; it's hard to visualize the longer term. Many married people develop dependencies, they cling devotedly to their obligations; they make a life for themselves but enjoy an underlying togetherness at times comfortable and reassuring, at times certain of their rightness for each other, at times bored with sameness and even disappointment, yet at times almost passionate about their feelings for each other. This is the way we live and marriage fits the pattern. It changes with us. That's why it gets better and/or worse and never stays the same. We make it work by remodeling it all the time.

CHAPTER
12

Family Life—
Too Rich a Mixture?

QUESTION: Isn't it true that the family today is under greater attack than ever?

ANSWER: Anthropologists have a saying, "Cultures are many; man is one." They mean, of course, that human nature is the same everywhere. We have the same problems others before us had even though we label them as unique and characteristic of our age. Some of the difficulties flare up more strikingly in one period of history than another but when we look more deeply, it's little more than the mode of expression which changes.

Our generation, for example, speaks of a gap between itself and its parents. Although they treat it as a discovery, a landing on the moon, it's more like unearthing the contents of Tutankhamen's tomb. The generation gap between parents and children has always existed. It's just that the flare-up is more vociferous today. But then, we talk more today about everything. We're freer to express ourselves, and our idiom and vernacular change more rapidly than ever. You needn't be a parent confronting your grown child to have difficulty in verbal communication. The age difference itself, no matter what the relationship, is enough. Nor is it merely the patois of our speech. Values have always shifted somewhat from one generation to another and today this change is accelerated at a pace more consistent with our supersonic age. It's hard to keep up, to keep in step. But then, older people have always referred to the good old days and younger people to the dazzling days ahead. Both parties stretch the gap and then wind up shaking their head in disapproval of each other. The human relationship most taxed by all this is what we endure in family life. Differences always lend themselves to judgment but nowhere so harshly as in families.

QUESTION: You mean we react more strongly to any difference of opinion in family life than we do elsewhere?

ANSWER: Absolutely. Consider the following illustration reported to me by a thirty-four-year-old man, married, the father of two children and a responsible executive of a large firm. His boss has a big confrontation with him about how he's been handling a major client. Their different points of view about the issues could cost him his job, but he stands firm, explaining the desirability of his approach, getting his boss to see that the small drop in sales came as a result of internal difficulties the client was having and were unrelated to his sales program for them. His boss grumblingly accepts yet leaves with the threat, "Well, okay, but it's your hide." Our protagonist remains confident and turns back to work with all his previous concentration.

Later in the day, he gets a call from his father who, after taking what seems forever to get through the ordinary amenities, begins to say, "Your mother's been hurt lately."

"Hurt by what?" asked impatiently.

"Well, you know. Your inattention."

"My what?" with rising irritability.

"She feels you never take the time anymore to tell her what's new."

"What's new? What the hell is new? She's on the phone every morning for half an hour with my wife. Wouldn't she learn then of the startling, history-making events which occur every day in our lives?"

"Now, Son, you needn't cuss and be cynical with me."

"Listen, Dad, I'm sorry. But I haven't got the time for this sort of thing—certainly not in the middle of a workday."

"Sure, Son, I understand. I'm sorry too. But maybe just the same you ought to take her out to lunch one day."

Ready to burst, "Dad, I've got to run. 'Bye. Okay?" What he wanted to say was, "When the hell was the last time you took her out to lunch? You're at the stage of life when you've got the time. Besides, the reason she claws at me is that *you* never did give her enough time. And Sis was smart enough to make her life three thousand miles away. As it is, I'm sick and tired of having her take up so much of Marge's time." But he controlled himself, remained minimally polite—only, when he turned back to work, he continued to steam inside and couldn't concentrate.

Notice how well he took in stride the realistic threats posed by his boss. He wasn't without feeling about them, but his feelings were crowded out by his objectivity and the sharpness of his thinking about the issues. Contrast this with what happens in his brief telephone conversation with his father. The issue is unthreatening and yet the feeling level expressed on both sides crowds out the better part of rational thought. The matter with his boss is over when the conversation ends. The feelings and emotions that arose in the conversation with his father go on long after its termination. In fact, there's a good chance that when he gets home he even tells his wife about it, still so upset that she has to calm him down. Not to exaggerate, it's very likely that much later in the evening or even the next day, he feels so guilty for his hostile thoughts that he actually does call his mother to chat with her. But he makes the call basically to assuage his own guilt, or at least prompted by it, and despite the fact that there's a large part of him that really doesn't want to make the call. Being conflicted, he turns out to be anything but nice on the telephone. Instead of being tactful and pleasant, he winds up getting into an argument with her. The whole fiasco begins to look like an unending spiral ever on the increase with no sight of a solution on the horizon.

QUESTION: You really think it's all that bad?

ANSWER: In more instances that I can count, it's even worse. I grant you I may have chosen a somewhat extreme example for the purpose of illustration, but I must assure you that this isn't at all atypical. The fact that you raise the question you do suggests that you yourself live a charmed life, that not all of your family experience is this negative. It's easy to grant because if it were all negative, the chances are families would have disappeared long ago. There's no question that family life can be very supportive and generally is to a large degree during the early years of the child. Much has been written about it, but very little appears in print about the grown child's relationship with his or her parents. This is strange because the fact is we don't merely grow up and live happily ever after. It's easy enough to find grown children who are more children than grown and it's equally easy to find parents who have failed to grow with their children.

QUESTION: But it can be and is, at times, good, isn't it, I mean, a family relationship?

ANSWER: I'm not waving a placard saying, "Down with the family." Not at all. When family life is good, it's very good, but when it's bad, it's very bad. It's easily given to extremes. Just as I've said elsewhere that I'm all for marriage and all for divorce, so also am I all for family life and all for nonfamily life. I'm basically interested in the individual and how he handles his emotional commitments. Let's take another illustration which I hope will lead us closer to some of the components of the problem.

Jill is an attractive woman of twenty-eight, unmarried but not at all upset by it. She dates a good deal, likes her job and enjoys a fair number of friends. She seems happy generally but periodically she goes into small tailspins, depressed moods in which she feels she hasn't accomplished anything in life, that she really hasn't done enough with herself. It was in one of these sad periods that I first saw her. Some interesting details of her life include the fact that only as recently as two years ago, when she was twenty-six, she finally stopped living with her parents and took a place of her own. "Mom and Dad still can't understand it. They keep reminding me that my beautiful room at home is still waiting for me with all the services thrown in—laundry, meals, everything. Why I should be spending so much of my earnings on a place of my own escapes them." It's interesting to note, too, that her first full-fledged sexual experience came only after she moved out of her parents' home.

"How often do you get to see or speak to your mother?" I asked. "Oh, I speak to her on the phone at least once a day, every day. We see each other several times a week." I wanted all that spelled out more fully and I learned that her mother still came by to deliver laundry she insisted on having done for her and food she insisted on shopping for, to mention only a few of the errands she performed.

"She still resents not having a key to my apartment so she has to come when I'm there to make the deliveries. I call her occasionally during the week but she calls me almost every morning before I leave for work and sometimes again in the evening."

Although I already expected what the answer would be I asked, "Do you buy your clothes alone?"

Jill blushed a little and explained what good taste her mother had.

"And you," I added, "also have great difficulty making up your mind, don't you?"

"How did you know that?" she asked.

"Because I suspect you never had much chance to," was my reply.

"I suppose you're implying that what I ought to do is *really* leave home."

"Well, in a sense, all you have is one foot out the door even though you have your own apartment."

It became clear to me that she would go into a blue funk because she hadn't in fact done enough with her life. She hadn't, even at the age of twenty-eight, become free enough to live it her own way. Her mother meant well but her love was controlling, almost asphyxiating. Unfortunately her love was not characterized by an ability to let go, to let her daughter make her own mistakes and find herself. Jill was bright and aware of all of this, but her insights alone were not enough to free her. Her periodic depressions were essentially a kind of mourning for all the things she never dared to do. She knew she couldn't feel fulfilled until she was free but her dependency stood in her way. She hated to buy clothes with her mother, for example, but she had become too dependent on her to do it herself. And this was true of many other aspects of her life as well.

With a large vote of confidence and gentle urging, Jill began to take the mincing steps necessary to transfer her dependence on her mother to herself and by doing more and more along these lines, it wasn't long before she could even say "no" gently to her mother and go her own way.

The point of the story is that despite the rivers of blood which have been shed in the cause of gaining our freedom in history, we easily allow ourselves to be owned. It's because we're children so long and are, in fact, dependent at the start of our life. Parents, in turn, don't easily see how they, too, become dependent on having children—so dependent, in fact, that many of them want their children always to remain children and dependent on them. The bona fide existence of dependency needs in children makes it even pleasant for us during that period of our life to lean on our parents, but dependency needs are discrepant with the demands of adult life, and make for conflict. Because we are children for longer than any other animal in the whole animal kingdom, whatever we do during that long childhood period of dependency easily becomes habitual. Long after we outgrow our dependency needs, the habit of being dependent can persist on its own, even in conflict with our need for freedom and independence. This conflict between our early needs which become long-standing habits and what we want as grown-ups not only causes friction between children and their parents but friction within us as grown children. It's as though different parts of us rub against each other with such force, a great deal of heat is bound to develop. Some people explode, others smolder quietly and others, like Jill, suffer periodic depressions because of their dissatisfaction with self. Whatever they do, their feelings are there, very much up front, occupying more of their attention than they would like.

QUESTION: There are grown men and women who get along with their parents better than all that, aren't there?

ANSWER: Of course there are. I was about to suggest that we look at still another example of a typical relationship along these lines. Once again the purpose of our illustration is to highlight some of the components of our life with father and/or mother. Consider the case of a man whose mother is well on in years, widowed, and both she and her son have strong positive feeling for each other. The man's wife is extremely considerate of her and sees to it that she's a frequent visitor to their home. What happens, however, on a typical weekend that she visits is that the man plays eighteen holes of golf on Saturday and Sunday part of the year, watches football on TV in the fall and winter and falls asleep watching. On Saturday night, he and his wife always have a date with friends. Their teenage children never seem to sit still long enough to have a conversation with anybody, including their grandmother. The man's wife spends somewhat more time with her, but is also drawn away by errands and chores which are all part of their daily life. Only once in a very long while does Grandma complain about how little time she actually spends with the grandchildren or her son and daughter-in-law on her visits.

But strange things happen anyway. The wife complains that her husband doesn't spend enough time with his mother and the man complains to his children that they don't spend enough time with their grandmother. And even without these complaints, there's a general awareness among the whole cast of characters that Grandma must be thinking that she's neglected by them even if she doesn't say anything about it. The result is that everybody is more irritated by her visits than pleased even though they're not going out of their way, changing their routine, doing anything different from what they ordinarily do. Her mere presence seems to spoil things for them.

Why? Because they feel guilty. Yet even when they want to spend more time with her, they can't. It just doesn't seem to work out and they are not entirely to blame. Their life-styles are light-years apart. A smart grandma would learn to watch football with her son in a strikingly knowledgeable way. She'd learn about popular rock singers so that she could talk animatedly about them with her grandchildren. She'd learn how she could be of help to her daughter-in-law without imposing herself on her. Being elderly doesn't necessarily mean one is infirm. Additionally, she must learn that to be treated well by her children, she must have an active enough social life of her own to be able to refuse them fairly often. There's a large difference in their feelings if they have to reach for her rather than feel they are essentially doing her a favor when they ask her to come visit them. But a lot of people feel that getting old is an invitation to giving up. Instead of living life, they want it to be served to them. This makes them dull and uninteresting, even if they are your parents.

It's the sense of guilt that I mean to highlight in this illustration. Despite all our laws and moral proscriptions, the place that guilt appears most commonly is in family life. The reason is that we're more involved, more committed than we are in any of our relationships in society at large. We may make contact with many people, but often it's little more than that. Rarely is there enough repetition and reinforcement of our feelings with others to match what happens at home. Sharing and dependency are hardly factors until we develop deep and meaningful friendships or fall in love. Even business partnerships today are more often than not corporate enterprises limiting not only financial liability but per-

sonal involvement between the parties. Our relationships in
the outside world have come to be so diluted that literature
abounds in descriptions of ours as an age of alienation, detachment and depersonalization. We become removed not
only from each other but even from our own feelings. The
impact made by sensitivity training came about largely in response to the needs created by this condition.

QUESTION: Doesn't this make family life all the more valuable to us?

ANSWER: Indeed it does. But I suspect the swing is too
great. On the one hand, our social relationships may not offer
us enough and on the other, our family relationships tend to
offer too much. One is too lean a mixture and one too rich.
In the illustrations given of family life between grown children and their parents, *dependency, hostility* and *guilt* have
been described as its prominent features. This is not to say
that love doesn't exist. It's just that it's all too often con-
taminated by these elements. Although love frequently fails
outside of marriage and family life also, it's extremely hard
for love to survive among members of one's family un-
burdened by dependency, hostility and guilt.

Take the parent-child relationship, for example. Not only
is it handicapped by a huge age difference but by an equally
huge bundle of dependency needs in the child. The incredible
amount a mother has to put out for a baby is almost always
enough to make her feel deserving of love, obedience and respect for the rest of her life. The child feels the love and attention of his mother but also feels pushed around a good deal.
He has to be taken care of and also has to be civilized so that
his behavior and not merely his appearance becomes identi-
fiably human. This isn't easy for either of them. Tensions between them invariably develop, spotting the affection they
might otherwise have for each other. Thus we all grow up
with varying amounts of affection and disaffection for our
parents and siblings. This division of our love and loyalty
between them and ourselves is virtually unavoidable and it's

highly charged with strong feelings and intense emotions.

QUESTION: Why is that? Is it absolutely necessary?

ANSWER: The reason is that we are constantly judged—morally judged—again and again and again. This is the major educational device used in families to teach children. Everything is either right or wrong, making us either good or bad. Bad means the withdrawal of love, which threatens the child with his parent's abandonment of his needs. Good means a guarantee that his parents will attend to his needs. These needs are very real to the child but often do not carry his parents' stamp of approval. As the child grows and begins to attend to his needs more and more by himself, parental approval and disapproval become an even bigger and frequently more irritating part of his life. He feels his own growth; his parents continue to feel the need for supervision. Parental control is certainly not surrendered when he believes it ought to be and in fact it goes on for many years.

QUESTION: I guess what you're saying is there's a lot of good and bad wrapped up in the parent-child relationship, isn't that so?

ANSWER: You're right. But I'm also trying to drive home the fact that with all this good and bad there's also considerable heat: feeling and emotion generated by the friction inescapably present between parent and child. After so many years of reactions of such intensity, habits form. These habits become part of us even long after we move out and no longer live with our family. We continue to overreact in response to them. The relationship has been fed so much—both good and bad—that it's safe to say we never become totally free of it. We never quite achieve a neutrality of feeling, an objectivity or an indifference that we achieve with others. We remain more easily bothered by things that happen even in the most occasional family contacts; we're often awkward in handling them and, worse yet, are easily given to feelings of guilt. Unfortunately, all this serves not only as a reminder of our earlier years but tends to keep alive the same influence on us.

QUESTION: I want to make sure I understand what you're saying. Is all this the result of our feelings of dependency, hostility and the guilt we suffered in the past in our family relationships? Is that why we continue to feel varying amounts of this later on?

ANSWER: Never underestimate the power of guilt. Historically, if not for the doctrine of original sin and the guilt it implanted in the minds and breasts of people, I daresay the incidence of rape and murder would have been ten times greater than it was. Police forces would have been larger than armies. Notions of right and wrong, good and bad, are so strongly drummed into us that after a while we don't need parents or other authority figures to judge or control our behavior. We keep ourselves in check. We develop a conscience, or a superego, as the psychoanalysts put it. In a sense, it's our own built-in police force which keeps us within the bounds of society. Out of it, we also develop our feelings of responsibility, duty, loyalty. Of course, it doesn't take us long to discover that all this conflicts with our desires. If we curb our desires we feel frustrated and angry about not getting what we want. If we act on our desires, we feel guilty for so doing. Either way we can't win, we can't get away scot-free. No, we pay a price either way. This is not to doubt the value of having both a brake and an accelerator with which to control our behavior. Having merely one without the other would make movement either impossible or dangerous. The trouble is that guilt slows us down to acceptable speeds by making us feel wrong, naughty, improper, *unworthy*. Nothing could be more damaging to our self-image. This is why I think of *guilt* as the dirtiest word in the psychological dictionary.

QUESTION: But you yourself said just a little while ago that we need restraints, a braking system. I imagine the world would be an even more unsafe place to live in than it presently is if people had no guilt. Don't you believe that's so?

ANSWER: I'm afraid you're right in at least one respect, namely that we're probably not far along enough in the whole evolutionary scheme of things to expect rational restraints to be reliable. But if we can stick with the problems of the individual rather than those of the race, the damage done by guilt might be too stiff a price for us to pay.

If we could stretch our imaginations a bit, it would be like having an automobile in which every time you stepped on the brake, your steering became stiffer and harder to manipulate until finally you could only drive your car in a straight line. People who have grown up with an overdose of guilt in their lives are very much like that. They wind up being that straight. They're easily threatened by the impropriety of the smallest deviation from anything they have been taught to believe is proper and correct. And as they judge themselves, they judge others too. They have less fun in life than is available to them and, being priggish, they resent a good deal of other people's fun. I like to believe there's another way—another way of achieving the control and direction and modification of our behavior, a way that doesn't make us feel wrong and unworthy or burden us with overcompensations such as dull feelings of self-righteousness.

I like to think that people of average emotional adjustment can learn by observing the consequences of their own behavior and recognize what is good or bad for them—the bottom line, or what works, replacing moral judgment. This is more natural to man. It's not at all a radical, new idea. Such an outstanding philosopher as Spinoza suggested it over three hundred years ago. It's not at all the childish, impulsive, let-it-all-hang-out notion that just because something tastes good, it is good. This idea suggests that something must not only taste good, but go down well, be digested and feel good when it's all over.

We got off the track somewhere in history and allowed people to tell us what was good or bad as they saw it through their own narrow, often ignorant and selfish needs. For centuries, for example, it was regarded as evil for a woman to enjoy sex; it was good for a man but not for a woman. Until recently, divorce was regarded as immoral and bad. There are countless judgments like these we still make, based on an outworn morality, not to mention social and economic conditions which no longer exist.

QUESTION: I know you're insistent on the value of recognizing how things work for us, that we see the effects of our own behavior on ourselves and then change it if it doesn't work. Does that mean that if a grown man or woman finds it irritating most of the time when he's with his father or mother that he stop seeing them, that he give them up?

ANSWER: It is one of the alternatives. It may even be necessary. As a rule, it's safe to say that it's best considered only as a last resort. The reason, quite simply, is that not seeing our parents is not the same as giving them up. We may avoid repeated confrontations with them, but we don't free ourselves of the guilt or even of our awareness of the fact that we can't handle them. Blaming them and avoiding them offer us no guarantee that similar things won't happen between us and others as we get close. Almost anybody denies this at first but later learns that he did not rid himself of early patterns of conduct by avoiding the people (his parents) who may have instilled them. In other words, even if our parents were initially totally to blame for our ineffectual, overemotional responses to them, our habits of response to them are not easily dissolved away. Worse yet, they can be incited by others with whom we develop strong emotional ties. Although many grown children are sick of it and want to stop trying to improve their relationship with their parents because they regard it as hopeless, it is nonetheless easier to do something about their own conduct *with them* than it generally is later on with others. There are very few people who have learned how to be happy if they have failed to do this. I repeat, unless we learn how to react like reasonably mature adults to our parents, instead of being repeatedly dragged into the childish maelstrom of emotional overreaction with them, we're not going to work out our intimate relationships later on. These include good friendships, one's marriage and ultimately one's own role as parent.

QUESTION: Well, okay, but how do you do it?

ANSWER: First by recognizing the importance of the job ahead of us. Second, it's equally important that we use our sense of anticipation. I've already pointed out elsewhere that if we wanted to, we could sit down tonight and write tomorrow's dialogue. We certainly can do this with our parents. We know them well enough to know almost exactly what their conversation is going to be as well as their responses to whatever we tell them. Why should we continue to react to them each time as though we were utterly surprised or dismayed by what they say or do? If we can predict their answers, we can prepare ourselves with appropriate responses which help us keep our cool.

The whole idea is not to pin their ears back or to vent our anger. What we ideally want to do is to reduce the overly rich emotional quality of our relationship because so much of it is negative. If we do this, we'll feel less dependent and less guilty at the same time. So, treat them well for the nice things they've done for us, but maintain a vigil for the emotional pitfalls and remain constantly ready for some plain and fancy sidestepping. Keep in mind that the best way to say "no" is with a smile. When we refuse them, we've got to make a joke of it as well. Let's keep in touch, touch home base from time to time, but let's not move in or overdo it. We must avoid a pattern so that our parents don't develop expectations and then disappointments when we don't stick to it. Try to be a friend rather than a son or a daughter—at least on a verbal and behavioral level. We mightn't feel friendly acting this way, but *the important thing is to do what works.* The feelings will come later. We'll find ourself developing controls we never believed we had. Our focus will be more on *our behavior* than on our disappointed and hostile feelings. Instead of

beating our breast and blaming our parents, we'll be con-
gratulating ourself on our skill and the lighthearted sense of
freedom it gives us. In fact, it won't be long before we begin
to recognize the application of these skills to our relationships with others. This is why this chapter is included in
this book!

QUESTION: Really? What do you mean by that?

ANSWER: The historic command "Clear the decks for action" is a relatively simple, straightforward one which (a) we
can follow and (b) actually helps prepare us for the action
that ensues. For us to clear *our* decks for action is a far more
complex matter. There are things we have to grow into and
things we have to grow out of. There's much for us to learn
and much for us to forget. Mostly, there's a great deal to
change. The history of our life in the family has been dominated by dependency, hostility and guilt. It's difficult for us
at best to change the patterns of feeling and conduct we develop out of these experiences. Growing helps because it gives
us the chance to do more and more for ourselves, but the
personal relationships between the principals in this drama,
namely parents and children, remain so close that earlier feelings between them easily overwhelm what we see and want
and expect of each other at the present time. This rivets us to
our childhood, keeping us from true maturity. Being grown-
up and a child at the same time makes it difficult for us
whether we are alone or with others. The deck that needs
clearing most is our relationship with the members of our
own family. Ordinarily we don't see it all that sharply. We
like to think we can walk blithely away from it. But that's like
trying to build two more sparkling modern stories on an old
house already shaky because of its weak foundation. If we are
going to fulfill ourselves in life, we need to free that self from
the now inappropriate past. This cannot be done merely by
fiat; a mere declaration of strong resolve doesn't do it. We
become free by working at it—working along the lines I've
just suggested. Even all this is a mere beginning. Still, working at it in this manner is the only effective way to begin living

our life with some expectation of making what we want of it.

QUESTION: I guess you believe that just as charity begins at home, so must our growth and maturity. Is that so?

ANSWER: It's the only way. Of course, human nature is so variable, almost anything can happen. But there are patterns of behavior in all of us and these patterns persist more often than not. This is what makes so much of our behavior predictable. We can count on unresolved feelings of dependency, for example, to show up in countless, troublesome ways later on in life. Take the case of Donna, who, at the age of thirty-two, has suffered through six absorbing love affairs, three of which involved broken engagements. On the face of it, these unhappy experiences seem unrelated to her inability to handle her parents with the skill described above. True, she gets upset very easily, as does her mother, whenever they talk or see each other. But what has that got to do with broken love affairs?

The point is that the strong feelings shared between Donna and her mother remain unresolved. They get upset, they shout, but they rarely work things out. Their feelings may be negative, but they're strong and they persist. Strong elements of dependency must be present also because it just goes on and on. Now, although anybody *wants* to fall in love, dependent people *need* to. So they do—only the closer they get to someone, the more dependent and demanding they become and the less able they are to resolve their differences without huge emotional cost. It's essentially a repetition of what happens with Donna and her mother, except that a boyfriend quits and a mother doesn't. Actually, Donna could have swung the other way and, just as she's critical and ineffectual with her mother, she might treat her lovers no differently until the relationship sours for them.

QUESTION: And the same happens with men also?

ANSWER: Absolutely. There are many men, for example, who overvalue the security of their job instead of recognizing their skills as the real basis of their earning power. They have the same kinds of irritating experiences with their boss as they had earlier in life—and maybe still—with their mother, but they stay on and on just the same. Even more common is the emotional overreaction of both men and women to each other and their children not only in their parents' homes but in their own as well. Negative feelings burst into angry confrontations of no corrective value. Again, at bottom it's our dependency feelings at work. The clue is in how much we want and demand from others. This is how dependency is most commonly expressed. Children, because of their dependency, are primarily the ones who can't take "no" for an answer. Yet how many of us, as grown-ups, act the same way, especially in our own home? Our emotional intensity and ineffectuality must tell us something about the basis of such behavior. Being right is an advantage, but it neither guarantees the result nor does it justify our behavior in the end.

It's a big step to go from wanting what you want to any modification of this such as wanting less, wanting something else, not wanting it at all. The step involves a big take-over—of your own life, putting yourself in charge of it. This helps you to become less dependent on having everything your way with the people around you. You see them for what they are, as they are. As they become part of the reality of your life, they initially seem somewhat less to you. You can no longer ask for what they don't have in sufficient abundance to give spontaneously. But what seems less at first soon grows into more. Only now it's realistic and lends itself to modification and improvement because your insight and skills are used instead of raw desire and feeling. We develop the ability to relate to our children and our parents as people, not merely as ours.

The possessiveness of the unimproved parent-child relationship invites and nurtures more dependency than is good for us in the long run. And this brings the worst out in us. It spills over into our dealings with people outside the home so that, without being aware of it, the closer we get to people, the more we expect from them even as friends, lovers or business associates. We all love the idea of surrounding ourselves with luxuries that are *ours*—of owning them. When it comes to material things, possession is what our dreams are made of. But it's a serious mistake to make ownership a condition for the love of people—even our own parents and children. It may be fine from the romantic point of view to tell your wife, "You belong to me." It's still better for her and you to treat her, not like a possession, but as a person like yourself. That is much closer to the reality of the relationship and leaves more room for true regard and love.

CHAPTER
13

How to Be Rich—
Inside

Certainly everyone wants to be rich. To refuse wealth is to raise questions of one's sanity for the simple reason that wanting is the psychological equivalent of breathing as a sign of life. So long as there's a breath left in our body, there's a desire to be found in our heart, and the easiest way to satisfy it is with money. Short of this, only the power of a divine-right monarch or military dictator compares. Otherwise, satisfaction demands some modification of desire. We have to learn how to make do, postpone, give up, compromise, rationalize, rediscover, substitute; in short, handle ourselves in a way that makes us less dependent on getting everything we want in order to feel good. This might seem to many like a sad alternative. But choose it we must, for few of us have the magic wand of unlimited funds. On the brighter side, however, we can all do more with what we already have *in ourselves.*

QUESTION: With what we already have in ourselves? What do you mean by that?

ANSWER: I mean our capacity to adjust, to bring what we

want into closer sync with the reality of what we get. To relate our hopes more realistically to the facts, to approach our opportunities (such as they are) with energy and ingenuity, to keep sharpening our overall sense of proportion and our awareness of how to work in our own best interests.

QUESTION: Wow! That's a big order.

ANSWER: Not really. That's what I mean by being rich—inside. I don't know how many people you know who have made millions of dollars. I've known a fair number and readily attest to the fact that financially, of course, they're far more secure than they were but . . . are they having more fun? Are they freer? Are they happier? Are they more easily satisfied than they used to be? Oddly enough, it takes *more* to satisfy them. Many, quite frankly, have grown old and mean. They're more easily irritated, more demanding, less compassionate: they tend to feel set upon, less understood; in short, on net balance, although they clothe and feed themselves more opulently and often *seem* much closer to being fulfilled and happy, they often aren't. They don't seem to be at any greater peace with themselves or the world.

QUESTION: You're not about to recommend sackcloth and ashes, are you?

ANSWER: Not at all. I deplore poverty. Go out and get rich if you can, but learn how to get rich inside as well. I'm suggesting that without this latter talent your material wealth might not be as fulfilling as promised.

QUESTION: Suppose it isn't. It's still pretty nice to have money. You know the old saying, "It's better to worry in the back seat of a chauffeur-driven limousine." I still feel if I'm going to be unhappy, I'd rather be rich and unhappy than poor and unhappy.

ANSWER: I agree. No one's arguing that. I have no brief

against wealth other than to recognize it for what I believe it is, namely one of our major resources in life, a means but not an end or goal in itself. It's a resource we can use to make the enjoyment of life easier. But we have other resources which are at least as valuable—good health, talent, charm or persuasiveness, imagination and still other inner resources which I call "rich inside."

QUESTION: Of course, I accept that. Particularly since my prospects for enormous wealth in the ordinary sense of the term are not great anyway. Where do we start?

ANSWER: With ourselves naturally. We take our ability to enjoy ourselves utterly for granted and focus almost exclusively on the value of having things to enjoy. The assumption we blindly make is that if we have the good things in life, we enjoy them and, just as the night follows the day, if we don't have them, there is little joy for us. The fact is the assumption is a lazy and uncritical one. It's a little too easy for most of us to explain away our sense of unfulfillment by the "slings and arrows of outrageous fortune." More commonly we have good breaks and bad breaks. Nobody's luck is *all* bad. There are countless people who have all of the ingredients for a good life and yet they never seem to get it off the ground. The reason is that, in addition to the external ingredients, we also need *the ability* to enjoy ourselves. A young woman, for example, meets the man of her dreams only to awaken to the reality that her irrepressible tendency to be questioning and critical gets in the way of her ability to enjoy her newfound love. A man gets the job he's wanted for years and soon discovers that he's working even harder than before and enjoying it less. Many people earnestly believe that when they get rich enough to ride around in a Cadillac and own a vacation home in the country, life will be sweet indeed. They discover to their chagrin that they remain just as irritable with traffic and the need for recurrent repairs of their automobile and that their weekend life in the country can be just as empty and boring as it was in the city.

QUESTION: I'm sure there are loads of people who don't enjoy what they have and I also know others who seem quite cheerful despite their very moderate circumstances. I think you're right. We do overlook *our ability* to enjoy things. What can we do about it? Isn't that a matter of temperament? Isn't it something we're born with?

ANSWER: Born with? No, a thousand times no. There are many experiences we have early in life, long before we know any better, which tend to predispose us in one direction or another, that is, to be cheerful or glum. An infant who has colic, for example, develops the same hunger pangs as a perfectly healthy child but finds that the process of satisfying his hunger, swallowing the food, is intensely painful. Getting what he wants turns out to be as distressing as not getting what he wants. Can you see how this can grow into an attitude of constant displeasure? This is, of course, an extreme example. But childhood is full of similar experiences. In fact, much of childhood is devoted to the very hard lesson that a great deal of what we like and gives us satisfaction is naughty and wrong. The measures taken to teach us this are often so oppressive, we learn more than was intended. We unfortunately also learn *not* to enjoy ourselves. For many people things have to be right, correct, proper, rather than just plain fun.

QUESTION: But what can we do about it? I don't mean to sound impatient, but when you get right down to it, it doesn't really matter whether we were born not to enjoy ourselves or simply developed the bad habit of not being able to enjoy ourselves because of the wrong kinds of experiences early in life. It all happened so long ago that it's almost the same as being born that way.

ANSWER: Not quite. The idea of being born in a certain way suggests a sense of resignation to what is and leaves little room for hope and change. Once we know that we *developed* these attitudes and expectations out of our early experiences, there's good reason to believe that different experiences could change all of that. The burned child, for example, can eventually learn *not* to dread the flame. The repeated experience of *never* being attacked by a large dog can certainly dilute one's fear of dogs. In the same way, people can be taught— better yet, they can teach themselves—how to enjoy themselves in situations they long dreaded. Learning how to swim, for example, changes one's feelings about the water. Learning how to ski makes the snow and heights far more acceptable. Learning how to dance or play bridge changes many a social situation from a dull or even threatening one to a decidedly pleasant one.

QUESTION: In other words, if you develop a skill that helps you use a situation, your experience with it will then be different, more enjoyable—yes, I guess that's it, more enjoyable. Is that how we develop the ability to enjoy things?

ANSWER: That's part of it. That's a very specific, concrete part of it which deserves another word or two. Much of this will be treated later on but for the present let us at least underscore the importance of the development of these abilities and interests in our life. The more things we learn to do moderately well and the more things we get interested in, the easier we make it for ourselves to enjoy life. One of the major reasons people find it dull and unpleasant to be with others is that they themselves have little to contribute. "All they do is talk about their problems or their children." But if we ourselves had more impelling interests and had developed conversational skills, we could ourselves direct the flow so that something else more interesting might be brought up. We don't enjoy people per se; we enjoy what we elicit from them. But in addition to our skills and interests, there's still another factor of even deeper importance involved in our ability to enjoy. I refer to what we think of ourselves. This image we have of ourselves is not necessarily all that sharp and clear. It cannot be written down as simply as our name, address and telephone number but emotionally it's a more important indication of where we're at. Some people, for example, are into themselves a great deal, involved in a constant tug-of-war with different parts of themselves. Life is a constant logjam for them, they're uptight, uncertain, uneasy. Others take themselves for granted. Their thoughts are directed outside of themselves. People and events command their attention. Being wrong doesn't carry with it an anti-Christ condemnation. They hang loose and enjoy themselves more easily.

QUESTION: Is this really the result of how we think of ourselves, that is, whether we hang loose or not?

ANSWER: I'm afraid so. You see, the person who thinks poorly of himself tends to be guarded, cautious, uncertain of acceptance, easily discouraged by his own performance. All of this adds up to being concerned with oneself, and the more concerned one is with self, the less attention he has for involvement with others. This is essentially a way of saying some people are freer than others—freer to enjoy themselves *through* others. Let me illustrate what I mean by choosing an overly simple and extreme example before we get on to more telling instances of the same thing.

If someone very dear to you were injured in an accident, it's highly unlikely that you would feel free to enjoy the excitement of the closely contested final game of a World Series while you paced the hospital floor waiting for news about your loved one. Granted this is extreme, as I said it would be, yet in more ways than we realize many of us are preoccupied even more constantly—if not so totally—in similar ways. A man, for example, who is short or who believes he has a smaller-than-average-size penis may be driven to prove himself in *any* activity, not merely sexual, no matter how trivial. The second, or middle child, of three children frequently falls into the same overly competitive position. When such people are fortunately endowed with the appropriate natural equipment, i.e. brains, physical coordination—this extra motivation or inner pressure to suceed often helps to make them champions. Even then, of course, the enormity of their intent and goals often crowds out the pleasure of the undertaking itself. But the fact is only a few people are extraordinarily endowed, leaving most of us striving for what we cannot achieve. Instead of relaxing and enjoying ourselves, we find our efforts constantly shadowed by disappointment, excuses and even unnecessary criticism of others.

QUESTION: I understand what you're saying, but aren't you still dealing with extremes? After all, how many short men are there, or middle children?

ANSWER: I must concede that you're right. Statistically they do not comprise the norm but they do represent it.

QUESTION: That sounds like a neat logical trick. Isn't it?

ANSWER: No, not really. You see, the way human nature works is much the same even at the extremes. The mental processes even of a psychotic are not totally different from those of a normal human being. There are differences to be sure but they're all within the same ball park. It's like the difference between pink and vermilion and, as a matter of fact, just as we can dilute or saturate colors so also do we, in therapy, dilute the harmful thoughts and feelings of the psychotic. We learn more about normal behavior from the study of the psychotic and more about the psychotic from the study of normal behavior. They both exist at ends of the same continuum. I grant you that the examples I've given so far are extreme in that they highlight what we're talking about, namely the things which bug us, which stand in the way of our ability to enjoy ourselves. At the extreme, we can see these things. But for most of us, they're much more subtle. All we see are the end results, namely that we're not getting as much of a kick out of things as we would like.

QUESTION: Okay. I'm sort of convinced but I still would like you to give me an example of what you just said, namely the case of the person who is not enjoying himself and who doesn't really know what's bugging him. Okay?

ANSWER: Fair enough. Remember we started this discussion by saying that how we think of ourselves is a major component of our ability to enjoy life. And we also said that we're not all that clearly aware of exactly how we think of ourselves. This makes it hard to illustrate, but I think you're right, I've got to try. Would you by any chance know any people who always see the downside of things? You can count on them to express the opinion that "we're heading for a terrible depression, there's going to be another war, there'll be no stopping inflation, the country's going to be riddled with strikes, the youth of the country have no future," and so on. The tone of their personal life is equally drab. Self-indulgence is viewed as a weakness unless you're a multimillionaire, and many of them act as though everyone's out to cheat them out of their money.

QUESTION: I do know some people who always see the dark side of things. Are you suggesting that their pessimism, which I suppose amounts to an inability to enjoy themselves, is the end result of something else that's bugging them— something which they don't even know?

ANSWER: I am indeed. After all, you and I look at the same things and see them quite differently, don't we? It isn't a matter of intelligence or knowledge of the facts of a situation; it's our emotional predisposition which bends us in one direction or another. One might reasonably ask how we get bent in one direction or another. How does the pessimist get to be the way he is?

Take the case of Tom P., an accountant whose income has been in six figures for the last twelve years. Not bad, eh? He has a nice wife, two children, a lovely home, many business associates and a fair number of friends. They tend to describe Tom at forty-five as successful, serious, highly dependable but, when you get right down to it, not terribly much fun.

Tom himself would agree that he's not very colorful or exciting. He puts it somewhat differently. "I've always had to work hard for whatever I got, but it pays off being this way. I don't take unnecessary chances and I never did have much time for the frivolous things in life. It was always that way as far back as I can remember it. My dad just managed to scratch out a living and Mom was a hard worker too."

All that's true, but only part of the story. It's the accountant talking, looking at the financial ledger of his life. It's harder for him to see the emotional ledger and it's there particularly that the red entries of his life can be found which have bugged him, handicapped him in his pursuit of happiness. He's not distinctly aware of it, but he was brought up to believe that life is hard, disappointment is the rule, the only thing you can count on is money in the bank. Essentially, he believed, there is no pleasure for people of my kind. Security, that is, financial security, is the best one can achieve. As a child, his homework came first, second and third, and after that, chores and responsibilities around the house. He failed to develop the skills to get along with his peers at school so that when he occasionally tried to have fun with them, it never seemed to work. Thus his parents seemed to be right. Getting good grades is better than being able to laugh with the boys or knock out a home run in a softball game ... well, maybe, but the latter soon became virtually impossible for him. So after a while he quit not only trying but even dreaming about it and threw himself more and more totally into his work. His goal became more and more sharply defined as *security* rather than *happiness*. The smallest departure from his strong addiction to this had become threatening for him. The fact is he now is what he is—what he was programmed to be. He's neither sick nor neurotic, he's competent, successful, but he simply never developed the skills necessary to enjoy his success. And there are many people like Tom.

QUESTION: It's true. It isn't that he has some strong, unconscious hang-up that keeps bugging him; he's just bugged by the values with which his parents raised him. But there are other people who are bugged by inner conflict, aren't there?

ANSWER: Absolutely. Take the case of Sheila M. Here's a woman who was brought up in an unhappy home, who almost couldn't help but become expert at acting out the unhappiness she got to know so well. Her mother and father fought constantly and were left emotionally drained by the force of their negative feelings. The children, she and her two sisters, received little or no affection. On the contrary, demands were constantly being made on them for more, for better—nothing they ever did was quite good enough. As they grew up, her two sisters, one older and one younger, got in trouble a good deal and were frequently punished. Sheila avoided this, or at least minimized the punishment she received, by a kind of quiet conformity to what was was expected of her. Even without being punished, however, she still never enjoyed a basic sense of self-worth because she never got any real praise, approval or sense of acceptability. She grew up as a responsible young lady holding a couple of good jobs until she married a young physician who saw her as sweet, sensitive, understanding—someone he could talk to and feel comfortable with—and different from so many of the spoiled young women he had dated—women who seemed only interested in good times.

As the years rolled by, his medical practice flourished, their two children were little or no trouble. Everything seemed right. The fact is he had been so busy and almost so totally preoccupied with his work that he had hardly noticed what was missing. Only when he took in a partner and began to work somewhat less did he begin to feel something was missing in their marriage and their life together. Yet he still didn't see it clearly. It's true his wife seemed devoted to him and the children; she was attentive, sensitive to their needs but always a little more worried, he felt, than she had to be. Even when they were out alone together—or when they gave a party—everything was just right but . . . come to think of it, there was little or no laughter. Whereas at one time he thought of his wife as mature, now he had begun to see her as prematurely old. What he thought was sweet, he now began to see as plain ordinary pessimism and unnecessary concern. Her health had become fragile for no physical reasons he could medically determine. Her sense of devotion to him began to resemble a cloying kind of dependency. Finally one evening while discussing a minor problem involving one of the children, he blurted out in a fit of impatience, "Damn it, it's always the same with you. You make mountains out of molehills. You always sound as if any minute the whole world's going to explode." Sheila not only burst into tears but sobbed uncontrollably for almost half an hour. It was clear even to her husband, a surgeon with little or no psychiatric background, that there was more here than either she or he had been aware of and that help was strongly indicated.

During the time Sheila got help, she learned even more sharply and painfully what little happiness she enjoyed even though everything had gone so well for her in life. She was constantly threatened with the fear that something would go wrong with her marriage, her children, her life. Nothing, for her, was ever good enough to guarantee things for her tomorrows. She never really felt free—free enough to give herself over totally to a situation. She never felt free enough to laugh. Her devotion to the details of life to keep them right was almost all-inclusive. It all looked good on paper but there was something missing. Her husband was right. But what she was depriving him of, she was depriving herself of. Only she hadn't quite seen it that way. The pattern of her behavior was so familiar to her and enjoyed such social approval, she saw nothing wrong in it.

QUESTION: And once she did and began to see clearly how much was missing in her life, was that enough to change it?

ANSWER: Not at all! As a matter of fact, it was painful for her to see this. It even added to her confusion initially. After all, she had worked very hard all her life to make things right for herself and then subsequently for her husband and children. Why should this be unrewarding? True, it took a lot of effort, more than it should—for what Sheila had failed to see was the reason for this effort. She had completely repressed her own feelings and desires out of fear of the consequences. She saw what both her sisters and her parents got for merely reaching for what they wanted. To avoid this, Sheila had come to assume that such desires didn't exist for her. But they did, deep down inside of her, and because they did she had to work so hard at being proper, correct, helpful to others and essentially self-denying. She *thought* she had what she wanted but she didn't *feel* that she had what she wanted. Discovering the conflict in the process of therapy was at first shattering. There's a big difference between the explanation of a condition and its cure.

QUESTION: That's what I want to know. What is the cure? What is the cure for Sheila and for the man, Tom, you spoke of a little while ago?

ANSWER: The therapeutic experience, as I define it, is an *experience,* not an *idea.* The effects on Sheila of having *experienced* punishment for acting on her desires when she was a child—or for witnessing the same in both of her sisters—can be changed only by providing a new *experience,* a whole host of new *experiences,* relating satisfaction, not punishment, to self-expression. After all, she isn't a child any more. She is now an adult and no longer needs permission to avail herself of the freedoms of a grown-up world. Her early negative experiences scared her and in remaining scared, she is acting in this regard still as a child. Now although we may adore freedom and opportunity, it's not all that easy for us to get rid of our own habits of enslavement—even in response to encouragement. But taking it in small doses initially, there's a good chance that Sheila would soon learn that if she acted like some of the young women her husband dated before his marriage to her—those young women who seemed to him at the time to be interested almost exclusively in good times—

she'd find that her husband would not bawl her out for being irresponsible. On the contrary, they'd both begin to have good times together.

The case of Tom is not essentially different, although the chances of his seeing a therapist are smaller because his unhappiness still hasn't generated specific symptoms. He too needs experiences the consequences of which would be pleasant for him rather than shattering, as he believes. This is the kind of man who, despite his years as a "good" husband who never ran around, is an odds-on favorite for the kind of extramarital affair that opens up the heavens and offers glimpses of greener fields, at least for a while. I'm not recommending this specifically because it can also be shattering for him and there are simpler ways to go about changing one's values.

QUESTION: I guess that's the nub of it: changing one's values, learning to see things differently. You're no doubt right about the fact that many of us have a great deal that we could be happy about but, as you say, we've lost *the habit of happiness.* How can we hold on to it?

ANSWER: If we could bottle it—or answer your question in a way that has a reliable effect on our behavior—I daresay it would be worth the richest of prizes. There really is no one simple answer, but there are answers. That's what this book is all about. The chapter on nasty habits or the one on needs we often neglect, as well as others, and this one in particular, all have to do with making life more palatable.

QUESTION: I appreciate your insights and your suggestions, but you also keep saying, "That's not enough in itself." You continue to emphasize how important it is for us to provide ourselves with the right kinds of experiences, to use your language, experiences which not only maintain our level of satisfaction but also help undo some of our early conditionings. Isn't that so?

ANSWER: It is indeed. Much as I'm fascinated by discoveries of *why* we fail to live life fully enough, I continue to see the utter lack of efficacy in the mere discovery itself. What I mean is that knowing isn't enough. It doesn't change things —unless we translate what we know into action. In other words, I can help you see *what's* wrong with your life and *why* it's wrong, but *you* have to provide the new experiences that can make things better for yourself.

QUESTION: I suppose that's what's meant when we say that, in the final analysis, we cure ourselves. But still, take the young man who's shy and has difficulty meeting women. So he forces himself, even against his own will, to go to some singles bars and finds the same thing all over again: either he can't talk to the women there or if finally he does, he's rejected anyway. How's that helpful?

ANSWER: When I say you've got to supply the new experiences, I don't mean to imply that any and all things you do are equally helpful—certainly not immediately. If the man you mentioned gave himself this new experience two or three times and then quit, I don't at all doubt that he'll feel worse than he even did before. In the first place, there are far more rewarding things he could do than to go to singles bars. And secondly, if that's all he did *but he persisted,* as opposed to remaining closeted in his own home night after night, even then changes for the better would take place.

QUESTION: But exactly what things might he do better than going to singles bars? After all, you can't just walk up to members of the opposite sex in the street and expect to start a conversation.

ANSWER: Remember, earlier I said that the process of increasing our enjoyment in life starts with ourselves. I like to think that if we make ourselves able enough, attractive enough, worthwhile enough, *people find us* no matter where we are—provided we are not actively withdrawing from them. Additionally, by doing these good things for ourselves we *feel* more worthwhile, so that it's a lot easier for us to relate to anyone. We rather enjoy putting ourselves in evidence if we have something to put in evidence. The point is that someone who doesn't have many friends—of either sex —is, in that respect, a loser. And he must feel like a loser. And feeling this way, he tends to act tentatively, fearfully, inadequately, unless he brashly overcompensates and does equally wrong things in the opposite direction.

QUESTION: But how does he break this pattern? Such a person strikes me very much like a dog chasing his own tail. How does he get out of the vicious circle?

ANSWER: Once again I must remind you that the answer is in what he does initially for himself. You see, when you speak of a man going to a singles bar in search of a woman, I believe you're misstating the problem. I don't doubt that he wants a woman but what he wants even more, more primarily, is a good time. He wants to be happy. There's no guarantee that a woman he meets there is going to help him become happy. She might in fact make him feel miserable. And that's something she can do easily because he already is miserable. He already feels awful and that's why he went there in the first place. Feeling awful, he doesn't have terribly much to give a relationship that he does develop. It's for this reason that it should all start with himself. First he's got to make himself feel a lot better; first he has to make himself happy. Only then can he brighten a relationship because he has something to give to it and, in that fashion, elicit some good from it.

QUESTION: But how can he make himself happy if he's miserable because he doesn't have a woman and you suggest that he do it without one? I find that difficult to follow.

ANSWER: Only because your diagnosis is incorrect. His unhappiness is the product only in small part of the absence of women in his life. There are many other things he can do to brighten his days and this, in turn, would make him a more attractive person. Instead of seeing him as a creep, women would find him more desirable. People no doubt are initially attracted to glitter, but what wears far better in a person is how interesting he is and how much he seems to enjoy himself. Often, at a party, some absolutely stunning young woman arrives and at first commands the attention of all eyes. Yet at the end of the evening, it's another woman who is surrounded by most of the men—not the most beautiful one, but the one who seems to be enjoying herself the most, the one who laughs the most, the one who is most responsive.

QUESTION: I see what you mean. It really does start with us. What are your recommendations on how I should get started?

ANSWER: I've always believed that a man is as rich as the number, quality and intensity of his interests—not the amount of money he has in the bank. It's all very simple. The more interests you have, the more sources of satisfaction you have and the more enthusiastic you are about them, the more you attract people to share these interests. This is the way *we* get to like people as well. We can't love our neighbor by command. We get to like people because of what we share with them, and out of this sharing comes not only a love of life but a respect for it and the people around us. Significantly enough, this is also the most effective way to improve our self-image.

QUESTION: You make it sound easy. Is that really the case?

ANSWER: I can't help but note the skeptical quality of your question and I must confess that it's well founded. *Of course all of this is a lot harder than it sounds!* The reason is that we're all lazier and more rigid than we like to believe. Repetition is the rule, not the exception, in our behavior. It's hard to get people to taste something they haven't tasted before, to listen to a new piece of music, to consider a new idea. It isn't that they can't. They won't. There was a time, as kids, when we didn't keep a checkbook and maintain a bank balance.

But we learned how. Maintaining our emotional balance is much the same. We needn't go to the trouble of making actual entries in a book, but we can benefit from frequent observations of how much we put out and what we get back in terms of satisfaction. We might, in this way, sharpen our understanding of what's important in life for our enjoyment of it. This brings us closer to acting in our best interests. On the bright side, I promise you it's hardest only at the start. The job gets easier all the time. As you develop social, physical, avocational skills as well as more and more interests—and grow enthusiastic about them—you'll discover that the process is self-reproducing. It goes on almost by itself with less and less effort on your part. These are the inner resources which constitute *emotional* wealth and help make life worthwhile. There's a keener sense of involvement and participation, we enjoy a greater degree of choice, our feelings of security increase with the satisfactions we reap, we always have more to give and more and more are glad to be ourselves.

QUESTION: That sounds great, but aren't you saying that the better adjusted we are, the richer we are inside? Aren't those one and the same?

ANSWER: It may look that way at first blush, but they really aren't identical. I don't think the concept of good adjustment tells the whole story. To be emotionally well balanced is unquestionably an enormous asset, but it often falls far short of great wealth. Anyone perfectly healthy, from a psychological point of view, can still be fairly bland, even dull, and miss much of the joy of exciting involvements. Without a cause—or, better yet, causes—being at peace with oneself may leave a man symptom-free and without conflict, but also without the tingle and thrill of "hard-fought" satisfactions. Good health—physical or mental—is an asset, I repeat, but only a very dull end in itself. The fact is we *suffer* the effects of poor health more than we *enjoy* the effects of good health. The latter *has to be used* to be fully enjoyed. And we use it by getting into things—things we deem important and enjoy. We don't—and can't—avoid frustration and disappointment entirely. Our good health helps us absorb these experiences. What we do avoid is boredom and hatefulness. And that means we're rich.

Index

About the Author

Dr. Fromme is primarily a clinical psychologist and therapist with over thirty years of experience in dealing with the emotional problems of the individual and his interpersonal relationships. In addition to his extensive private practice and clinic experience, he has taught psychology at Columbia University, Sarah Lawrence College and the College of the City of New York. He has lectured widely in the East and the South, and has written six books which have been translated and distributed throughout the world.